FEELINGS DON'T CARE ABOUT YOUR FACTS!

How Emotional Reasoning Hijacks Logic

Dr Chuck Carrington

This is a nonfiction work. However, certain sections have been lightly fictionalized or dramatized for illustrative purposes. Any resemblance to actual persons, living or deceased, is purely coincidental.

Disclaimer:
This book is not intended to diagnose, treat, or cure any psychological or medical condition. It is for educational and self-reflective use only. Any strategies, stories, or suggestions are offered as general guidance and may not be appropriate for all readers. If you are experiencing persistent emotional or mental health difficulties, please consult a licensed professional. The author and publisher assume no responsibility for actions taken based on the content of this book.

Copyright © 2025 CP Carrington
all rights reserved
ISBN 979-8-9892386-7-5 (paperback edition)
Printed by Connect Books in the United States of America

CONNECT BOOKS
USA

PO BOX 903 Wakefield VA. USA 23888
Connectbooks.pub

All rights reserved. No part of this book may be reproduced in any form or by an electronic or mechanical means, including information storage and retrieval systems, without permission in writing from the publisher, except by a reviewer who may quote brief passages in a review.

DEDICATION

To all of those clients, friends, and family who have shared with me their frustration in balancing their love, their needs, and their faith when trying so hard to maintain a relationship in crisis, this book was written with all of you in mind.

Acknowledgements

To Larry Mast—without his sharp eye and steady editorial guidance, I'd still be lost in a dyslexic fugue of doubt. I am deeply grateful.

-and-

To the men of and women who volunteered to be the readers of the raw book, thank you for slogging through my ramblings!

Contents

Why This Book Should Matter to You 5
A Storm in Their First Year 7
The Hijacking of Reason by Emotion 11

Part 1 Emotional Dysregulation 17
   Chapter 1 The Grip of Emotions 19
   Chapter 2 Shaping Thoughts 37
   Chapter 3 Emotional Reactivity 53

Part 2 The Roots of Emotional Dysregulation ... 67
   Chapter 4 Family Dysfunctions 69
   Chapter 5 Betrayal Trauma 81
   Chapter 6 Perspective Taking 87

Part 3 Healing Emotional Dysregulation 99
   Chapter 7 Emotional Awareness 101
   Chapter 8 Finding Calm Within 109
   Chapter 9 Healing Betrayal 149
   Chapter 10 Building Resilience 167

Part 4 Maintaining Healthy Relationships 187
   Chapter 11 Beyond Survival 189
   Chapter 12 Trust in Marriage 209
   Chapter 13 Loving the Dysregulated 223
   Chapter 14 Trust in Parenting 235
   Chapter 15 An Emotionally Regulated Family .. 245

Part 5 Long-Term Healing and Growth 259

    Chapter 16 Shame and Self-Sabotage 261

    Chapter 17 A Personal Healing Plan 275

Part 6 Summing the Parts 285

Part 7 Grounding and Coping Strategies 299

FORWARD:

I want to begin this book with an admission—one that shouldn't need to be said, yet I feel compelled to say it anyway: It is crucial to recognize when you are *not* the smartest person in the room. I learned this lesson firsthand when transitioning from my master's program to a doctoral program, where I found myself surrounded by faculty and peers whose intellect was, frankly, staggering.

From the outset, I bow to the brilliance of Mr. Ben Shapiro. My purpose in writing this book is not to refute, correct, or diminish his views in any way. In fact, I regularly use his declaration and motto "Facts don't care about your feelings"[1] in my counseling practice, because it is true. Instead, my goal here is to use his insights as a springboard to explore a struggle that ordinary people—especially spouses—face daily. Despite the power of facts and logic, there are moments when reason alone is not the tool required. In those times, understanding and wisdom must take precedence to create space for healing, or at the very least, to sustain relationships amidst emotional dysregulation and chaos.

So, to my fellow Ben Shapiro fans—among whom I count myself—please know that this book is written not in opposition, but in appreciation, seeking to apply truth in the most human and relational way possible.

Introduction:

Emotional dysregulation—the inability to manage and respond to emotions in a healthy, balanced way—can quietly shape a person's entire life. It affects how we think, how we relate, and how we respond to stress. For many, it begins early—rooted in childhood experiences like trauma, neglect, foster care, or growing up in a dysfunctional home. For others, it emerges later through betrayal or repeated emotional wounds. Whatever the origin, the result often feels the same: an invisible weight that makes normal interactions feel overwhelming.

And when emotional dysregulation takes hold, it often gives rise to relationship dysfunction—a pattern of unhealthy interactions where communication breaks down, trust is weakened, and emotional needs go unmet. Over time, individuals and families can find themselves stuck in cycles of conflict, disconnection, or emotional shutdown.

This book is about that experience—and how to heal from it. When someone is emotionally dysregulated, it's not just about being "too sensitive" or unwilling to reason. The brain is often stuck in survival mode, making it incredibly hard to process logic, truth, or differing perspectives. What might look like overreaction from the outside is often a deeply ingrained response pattern on the inside.

But here's the hope: these patterns can change. By tracing emotional dysregulation back to its roots, recognizing how it shows up in daily life, and walking through a clear and structured path toward healing, transformation is possible. In the pages ahead, we'll combine clinical insight with practical tools and a biblically grounded framework. Whether you're reading for yourself, your marriage, or your family, you'll find guidance here for building emotional resilience, restoring connection, and living from a place of greater peace and stability.

Why This Book Should Matter to You

Emotional Reasoning Destroys Love

If you are in a relationship, and conflicts are constant, heated, or often take you and your partner to a place of hurt and resentment, chances are one or both of you are falling into the trap of emotional reasoning. Emotional reasoning creates a no-win situation where things are said, ultimatums given, or actions are taken that you or your partner really don't mean or have no intention of backing up. They are said to stop the fight, or to win the battle. But, like nuclear weapons, emotional reasoning tactics are weapons of mass destruction that cannot be undone, leave long term effects, and will eventually kill the relationship over time. Like radiation seeping into your relational environment, emotional reasoning toxifies your relationship. The result is relationship dysfunction and relational distancing. Empathic wounds abound, and little by little, the cancer of resentment rots the soul. By understanding the process of emotional reasoning, you and your partner can begin to halt the use of this weapon of mass destruction, then, with some deeper understanding, begin to disarm. Disarmament is done through self-exploration. Childhood trauma, dysfunctional family conditioning, past failed relationships, betrayals, and current relational failures with their own empathic wounds all build your weapons. Understanding these will help you defuse and dismantle them. Once disarmament is achieved, peace and a healthy love story can prevail.

The Process in the Book.

In this book, we start here in part one with the current reality of the conflict, through some scenarios to demonstrate what emotional reasoning and empathic wounding looks like. Then, in part two, we will examine the nuts and bolts of emotional reasoning and the way the brain acts and reacts during conflict or perceived trauma threats. In part three, we will look at underlying common causes for habitual reliance on emotional reasoning, usually found in past experiences. In part four, we will move on to coping and overcoming using various grounding techniques, self-help strategies, and collaborative strategies you and your partner or loved ones can join in. And finally, in part five, we will discuss how to manage relationships in the presence of ongoing relapses into emotional reasoning events, with the acceptance and understanding that old habits and coping strategies die hard. By the end of the book, you will be an expert on the nature, process, and techniques for dealing with your own or your loved one's emotional reasoning, so that you do not get trapped in the cycle between facts and feelings since, in the heat of the argument, despite all logic, *Feelings Don't Care About Your Facts!*

A Storm in Their First Year

The dinner plates clinked against the countertop as Emma stacked them, her movements sharp and deliberate. The apartment was small, but the tension between her and Ryan filled the space like a thick fog, heavy and inescapable. She had asked him—no, told him—two days ago to pick up the special lavender-scented laundry detergent she loved. It wasn't just a preference; the scent reminded her of safety, of the few moments in childhood when her grandmother held her close, her cardigan smelling like dried lavender and warmth. She had made it clear how important it was. But Ryan had come home with a different brand. Unscented. "They were out of the other one," he had said casually, tossing the bottle onto the counter.

At first, she had swallowed her irritation. It was just laundry detergent, after all. But then, as the evening passed, the thoughts began creeping in. *Did he even listen? Did he even care?* She had told him how much it mattered to her. If he couldn't even remember something so small, what did that mean about the big things? By the time the argument started, it wasn't about detergent anymore. "You never listen to me, Ryan!" Emma's voice shook as she stood in the middle of their tiny kitchen, her fists clenched at her sides.

Ryan rubbed his temples. "Emma, it's detergent. They didn't have the one you wanted. I got the closest thing. How is this such a big deal?"

"It's not just this!" she spat back. "It's everything! I tell you what I need, and you ignore me. Do you even care about what I want?"

His brow furrowed, his confusion deepening. "Of course I care! But, Emma, this is irrational. You're blowing this out of proportion."

The moment the words left his mouth; she felt a fire ignite in her chest. *Irrational?* She had heard that before. As a child, when she cried too loudly. As a teenager, when she tried to tell her mother how lonely she felt. The message was always the same: *Your feelings are too much. You are too much.*

Her voice turned sharp. "Irrational? You think I'm crazy, is that it? That I'm just making things up?"

Ryan groaned and ran a hand through his hair. "That's not what I'm saying! I just think you're letting your emotions take over. I need you to stop for a second and think. Just calm down—"

She let out a bitter laugh, the sound hollow. "Calm down? Oh, I see. I get upset, and suddenly I'm the problem. Maybe if you actually cared, I wouldn't be so upset in the first place!"

Ryan's patience was thinning. "Emma, this isn't fair! You're making this into something it's not. I made a mistake, okay? I didn't realize it was that important, but now I do. Why are you acting like I did this on purpose?"

His words weren't landing. She was too deep in it now. The fear, the shame, the crushing certainty that he didn't really care—not in the way she needed.

She shook her head, eyes burning. "Because this is what you do, Ryan. You dismiss me. You make me feel like I don't matter."

"That's not true!" he shot back, his voice rising now. "God, Emma, you're twisting everything I say! I'm trying to talk to you, but you're not even hearing me."

Emma felt herself unraveling. She wasn't hearing him?! He wasn't hearing her! *He was the one not listening!*

Her voice dropped, slow and sharp like a knife. "Maybe I was wrong about you. Maybe I thought you were different."

Ryan's expression went blank, his lips parting slightly in shock.

"What does that mean?" he asked, his voice quieter now, like he wasn't sure he wanted the answer.

She folded her arms. "It means if this is how you treat me now, I don't even want to know what the next five years will look like."

The words hung in the air like a bomb, and she saw the way his face changed, something inside him closing off. His jaw clenched, and his eyes, which had been filled with frustration, now held something else—hurt.

"Wow," he whispered, shaking his head.

She turned away, crossing her arms tightly over her chest as she stared out the window. Her body trembled, not from anger now, but something deeper, something unspoken. Behind her, she heard the sound of his keys jangling. Her stomach dropped.

"Where are you going?" she asked, her voice suddenly small.

Ryan let out a breath, shaking his head. "I don't know. I just—I need to get out of here for a bit."

Panic surged through her veins, but she fought to keep her voice even. "Oh, so now you're leaving?" she snapped. "Great. Real mature, Ryan."

He gave her one last look—one she couldn't quite read. Then, without another word, he grabbed his jacket and walked out the door.

As soon as it shut behind him, the tears came. She collapsed onto the couch, gripping a pillow like it was the only thing holding her together. Her mind screamed at her: See? He left. Just like everyone else. The logical part of her, buried somewhere beneath the weight of her past wounds, whispered: *But you pushed him away.*

She didn't know which voice to believe.

The Hijacking of Reason by Emotion

Emotions are powerful, deeply embedded mechanisms designed to protect and guide us, but when unchecked, they often lead us into irrational territory. The phrase "feelings don't care about your facts" encapsulates a fundamental reality about human cognition—when emotionally activated, individuals struggle to engage in logical reasoning or perceive the intentions of others accurately. Instead of operating from the rational, prefrontal cortex, the emotionally overwhelmed individual defaults to the limbic system, where survival instincts reign.

John Bradshaw[2], in his works on family dysfunction and emotional wounding, laid a foundation for understanding how arrested development exacerbates this issue. The immature, wounded self—the inner child—reacts impulsively, often interpreting neutral or even supportive interactions as threats. This chapter will explore how emotional reasoning emerges from arrested development, distorts relational interactions, and turns allies into perceived adversaries.

Emotional Reasoning: The Inner Child's Voice

Emotional reasoning is the cognitive process of interpreting reality through the lens of feelings rather than objective evidence. If a person feels abandoned, rejected, or threatened, they believe those perceptions to be reality, even in the absence of supporting facts. Emotional reasoning is a key feature of arrested development, where unresolved wounds from childhood continue to dictate adult reactions.

The Role of the Inner Child in Emotional Reasoning.

The inner child is the repository of early experiences, especially those laden with pain, rejection, or neglect. When a person experiences conflict, the inner child often emerges, taking control of perceptions and reactions. Instead of responding with the rational, mature self, they regress to earlier patterns of emotional survival.

For example, an adult whose needs were neglected as a child may interpret a spouse's busyness as intentional neglect. Even if their partner offers explanations or reassurances, the emotional self clings to the childhood narrative: "I am not important. I am not loved." This emotional belief overrides any logical reasoning, leading to conflict escalation.

The Brain on Conflict: Why Logical Reasoning Shuts Down

The Prefrontal Cortex vs. The Limbic System. In a non-emotional state, the prefrontal cortex—the part of the brain responsible for reasoning, problem-solving, and impulse control—manages responses. However, during moments of heightened emotional distress, the limbic system, particularly the amygdala, takes over. This phenomenon, known as ***amygdala hijacking***,[3] prevents logical thought and instead triggers a fight, flight, or freeze response.

Perceiving the Other as an Enemy

When emotional reasoning dominates, people no longer see their conversation partner as an ally but as an adversary. This shift occurs because:

- The brain misinterprets disagreement as a personal attack.
- Past wounds resurface, coloring present interactions with historical pain.
- The emotional self equates vulnerability with danger, triggering defensiveness.

For instance, a husband attempting to discuss finances with his wife may trigger her deeply rooted fear of insecurity from childhood. Instead of engaging in a problem-solving dialogue, she may lash out, believing he is controlling or criticizing her. Her reaction is not based on the current conversation but on an emotional wound that distorts her perception.

Emotional Distancing: The Destructive Coping Mechanism

Avoidance as a Defense Against Emotional Overload

One common reaction to overwhelming emotional reasoning is emotional distancing. When individuals feel too vulnerable, they withdraw, avoiding meaningful engagement. While this may temporarily prevent conflict, it ultimately deepens relational fractures.

Signs of Emotional Distancing

- Stonewalling or shutting down in conversations
- Using sarcasm or humor to deflect serious issues
- Becoming overly logical or dismissive of emotions
- Engaging in passive-aggressive behaviors instead of direct communication

Bradshaw's work highlights how unresolved emotional wounds cause people to create protective emotional barriers. These barriers prevent the very intimacy and connection that healthy relationships require.

The Fallout of Emotional Disruption in Relationships

How Emotional Reasoning Breeds Conflict

When one or both partners engage in emotional reasoning, conflicts become cyclical and unresolvable. Instead of seeking resolution, the emotional self seeks validation of its pain, often through blame, escalation, or withdrawal.

Common patterns include:

- Blame-shifting: "If you hadn't said that I wouldn't have reacted this way."
- Mind-reading: "I know what you really meant by that comment."
- Victim mentality: "You never care about how I feel."

The Role of Confirmation Bias

Once emotions dictate perception, confirmation bias strengthens the belief that the other person is the enemy. *Confirmation bias* is the tendency to notice and believe only the information that supports what we already feel or assume—while ignoring anything that might challenge that view. Every action, word, or omission is then scrutinized for evidence that fits the wounded self's narrative, reinforcing a sense of betrayal or hostility even when it may not be accurate.

Healing Emotional Reasoning: Cultivating Self-Awareness and Regulation

Step 1: Recognizing Emotional Hijacking

The first step toward healing is acknowledging when emotional reasoning is taking over. Signs include:

- Reacting strongly and disproportionately to a situation
- Feeling unable to listen objectively
- Experiencing overwhelming feelings of rejection or betrayal

Step 2: Engaging the Prefrontal Cortex

To counter emotional hijacking, individuals must re-engage their rational brain. This involves:

- Pausing before reacting – Taking deep breaths or stepping away before responding
- Asking clarifying questions – "What did you mean by that?" instead of assuming intent

- Reframing thoughts – "Could there be another explanation?"

Step 3: Practicing Emotional Repair

Emotional repair is the process of acknowledging the damage caused by emotional reasoning and actively working to mend relational ruptures. This includes:

- Apologizing for reactive behaviors – "I realize I overreacted. I'm sorry."
- Seeking understanding – "I think my reaction came from an old wound. Can we talk about it?"
- Offering grace to one another – Recognizing that both partners carry emotional baggage

Choosing Emotional Maturity Over Emotional Reactivity

The reality that *feelings don't care about your facts* is not an indictment of emotion but a call to greater emotional maturity. Emotional reasoning, while deeply ingrained, does not have to control our lives or relationships. By recognizing when our emotions hijack our rational mind, engaging in self-awareness, and choosing to see our partners as allies rather than enemies, we move toward healthier, more fulfilling connections.

John Bradshaw's [4]work reminds us that emotional wounds do not heal by accident; they require intentional reflection, engagement, and re-parenting of the inner child. When we step out of emotional reasoning and into emotional responsibility, we reclaim our ability to navigate conflict with wisdom, love, and grace.

Part 1
Emotional
Dysregulation

Emotional dysregulation—the inability to manage and respond to emotions in a healthy, balanced way

Chapter 1 The Grip of Emotions

Chapter 2 Shaping Thoughts

Chapter 3 Emotional Reactivity

Chapter 1
The Grip of Emotions

Navigating Emotional Dysregulation: Reclaiming Control Over Your Reactions

Imagine yourself at sea in the middle of a storm. The waves crash unpredictably, tossing your small boat in every direction. You have no control over the water, no way to steady yourself, and no clear path to safety. This chaotic environment is what it feels like inside when you struggle with emotional dysregulation. It's not just about feeling strong emotions—it's about struggling to manage them in a way that fits the situation. Unlike typical emotional responses that come and go, dysregulated emotions can completely overpower your rational thought, leading to impulsive reactions, irrational fears, and relationship conflicts.

Trapped on the Roller Coaster

You wake up expecting a normal day, but the smallest inconvenience—maybe someone forgot to replace the milk—sets off a flood of frustration. Moments later, that frustration shifts into sadness, and suddenly, you feel emotionally drained before the day has even begun. You recognize that your reaction is bigger than the situation warrants, but the emotions are so intense that ignoring them feels impossible.

This rollercoaster of emotions is a daily reality for those dealing with emotional dysregulation. The shift from anger to despair, from excitement to exhaustion, can happen in an instant, sometimes without a clear reason. To others, your emotional swings may seem excessive or irrational, but to you, they feel completely real and overwhelming. It's as if your emotions have taken control of your life, steering your actions without your permission.

Emotional dysregulation keeps you from returning to emotional balance as quickly as others might. While some people can shake off stress and move on, you might feel like you're wading through knee-deep mud, struggling to regain a sense of calm. Minor frustrations feel like personal attacks. A misunderstood text message from a friend or a bit of unexpected criticism at work can trigger a tidal wave of emotions—anger, anxiety, shame—all crashing down at once. In these moments, logic takes a backseat, and your emotions drive the narrative, drowning out reason. The intensity of your response isn't just about what's happening in the present—it's a flood of unresolved emotional wounds surfacing all at once.

Imagine being caught in a storm without an umbrella, without shelter, with no way to tell when the rain will stop. This is what it feels like when you lack self-soothing skills. When emotions become overwhelming, you may struggle to bring yourself back down. Instead, you might look for external relief—seeking reassurance from others, numbing your emotions with unhealthy habits, or withdrawing completely. Without effective coping tools, your nervous system remains in a heightened state of distress, leaving you feeling powerless over your emotional world.

Impulsivity: When Emotions Take Over Your Actions

Impulsivity is another defining trait of emotional dysregulation. Picture yourself in the middle of an argument, your anger flaring like a match catching fire. In that heated moment, you say things without thinking—words meant to wound, not resolve. Later, when the emotional storm has passed, regret settles in. But by then, the damage is done. Your relationships suffer, your career takes hits, and a cycle of guilt and shame keeps repeating itself.

One of the hardest parts of emotional dysregulation is the tendency to see the world in black and white. Someone is either completely trustworthy or a total betrayal. A mistake at work means you're either a success or a complete failure. This kind of thinking leaves little room for nuance or grace. Relationships become fragile—every disagreement feels like an irreparable break, and every disappointment turns into proof of your deepest fears.

Where Emotional Dysregulation Begins

At the heart of emotional dysregulation is often a history of unresolved pain. Maybe you grew up in a home where emotions weren't acknowledged, where you had to fend for yourself emotionally. Maybe past relationships left you feeling abandoned or unheard. Whatever the cause, your nervous system has learned to stay on high alert, interpreting everyday stressors as serious emotional threats. But here's the truth: this isn't your fault. Emotional dysregulation isn't a personal failure—it's a learned response, shaped by your experiences. And the even better news? Healing is possible.

If this feels familiar, you're not alone. Emotional dysregulation is not a life sentence. You can learn to regain control over your emotions, build self-awareness, and develop skills that bring stability to your life. In the chapters ahead, we'll explore how to move from being controlled by emotions to gaining control over them—building self-awareness, strengthening emotional regulation skills, and ultimately, finding peace in a world that once felt overwhelming.

Picture this: You wake up late. Your alarm didn't go off—or maybe you hit snooze too many times. Now, you're scrambling to get ready, rushing through your morning routine, your heart pounding as the minutes slip away. You barely have time to grab a cup of coffee before heading out the door. Then, just as you're about to leave, your partner makes a comment—something small, maybe about how you always seem to be in a hurry.

And suddenly, something shifts inside you…

That one comment, harmless to an outsider, feels like an accusation. A flood of emotions rises—frustration, hurt, maybe even shame. Before you know it, you're snapping back with a defensive remark. They respond, their voice tense now, and just like that, the morning has spiraled into an argument. What started as a rushed morning has now become something much heavier, something that lingers long after you've walked out the door.

For you, this isn't just a bad morning—it's a pattern. Small frustrations don't stay small. Instead, they snowball, turning into full-blown emotional crises that leave you feeling drained, misunderstood, and, at times, ashamed of how quickly things escalated.

When Small Triggers Become Emotional Landmines

It's not just in your personal relationships, either. At work, a simple critique from your boss can feel like a personal attack. The logical part of you knows it was just feedback, but your emotions tell a different story. A single comment can lead to hours of self-doubt, replaying the conversation over and over in your head, convincing yourself that you've failed entirely.

Social interactions become minefields. A friend doesn't respond to your text right away, and suddenly, a wave of anxiety rushes in—*Are they upset with me? Did I say something wrong?* Instead of brushing it off, the uncertainty gnaws at you, pulling you into a cycle of overanalyzing and worrying.

Even the simple act of making plans can trigger emotional upheaval. If something gets canceled unexpectedly, disappointment morphs into resentment, and you're left wondering why everything feels so personal, so intense. Rationally, you might understand that plans change, that people get busy, that not every comment is meant to hurt you.

But emotionally? It feels impossible to separate what is happening from how deeply it affects you.

Recognizing the Patterns of Emotional Dysregulation

Emotional dysregulation affects multiple areas of your life, influencing the way you process emotions, interpret interactions, and navigate the world around you. These patterns are not just momentary reactions; they shape your experiences, relationships, and self-perception in profound ways. Recognizing these tendencies is the first step toward regaining control over your emotional world.

How You Process Emotions: When Every Feeling Feels Too Big

You may struggle to regulate intense emotions, making even minor stressors feel overwhelming. Instead of experiencing emotions in a manageable wave, you might feel as if they hit like a tidal surge, drowning out logic and balance. What seems like a small inconvenience—getting stuck in traffic, misplacing your keys, or receiving constructive criticism—can ignite an emotional firestorm, leaving you feeling frustrated, anxious, or even devastated.

Instead of emotions rising and falling naturally, they may linger for hours or even days, keeping you locked in a state of distress. Your nervous system stays on high alert, making it difficult to find calm after a triggering event. Even when you logically understand that your reaction may be disproportionate to the situation, the emotional intensity remains just as real and consuming. This makes self-soothing difficult, leading to a cycle where emotions dictate your decisions, reactions, and sense of well-being.

How You Interpret Interactions: When Neutral Situations Feel Like Attacks

Your brain may automatically assume the worst, perceiving neutral situations—or even well-intended interactions—as threats. A simple delay in response from a friend might feel like rejection, triggering anxiety that they are upset with you or no longer value the relationship. A routine email from your boss might suddenly seem like a sign of impending failure, causing self-doubt to spiral out of control.

Instead of being able to pause and assess the situation with a balanced perspective, your brain may jump to conclusions that reinforce deep-seated fears—fear of abandonment, fear of failure, fear of not being enough. These emotional reactions are often rooted in past experiences, where similar situations may have led to real pain or rejection. However, your brain may now overgeneralize, treating every uncertainty as confirmation that something is wrong.

As a result, you may find yourself overanalyzing conversations, searching for hidden meanings where none exist. A casual comment from a loved one might feel like a criticism, or an unreturned text might feel like proof of being ignored or forgotten. These perceptions, though deeply felt, can distort reality and make it harder to engage in healthy, secure relationships.

How You Move Through the World: When Emotions Dictate Your Life

Your emotions may feel like they control everything—your relationships, your career, and your overall sense of self-worth. Instead of feeling grounded in who you are, you may find yourself bouncing between extremes, feeling deeply confident one moment and completely inadequate the next.

In relationships, this emotional intensity can create patterns of clinging too tightly or pulling away entirely. You may seek constant reassurance from loved ones, fearing abandonment even when there's no real threat. Or you may avoid emotional closeness altogether, believing that distancing yourself is the only way to protect yourself from pain. This instability can make relationships feel like a constant struggle, leading to tension, misunderstandings, and unmet needs on both sides.

In your career, emotional dysregulation can make handling feedback, criticism, or uncertainty extremely difficult. A simple suggestion from a supervisor might feel like a personal attack, leaving you questioning your abilities or feeling like a failure. You may hesitate to take risks, fearing that any misstep will confirm your worst fears about yourself. Alternatively, frustration may drive impulsive decisions—quitting a job suddenly, sending an angry email, or withdrawing from professional opportunities because emotions feel too overwhelming to manage.

Your self-worth may also feel fragile and dependent on external validation. When things are going well, you might feel on top of the world, but the moment something goes wrong—a mistake, a perceived rejection, a bad day—your confidence crumbles. Instead of seeing challenges as part of life, they may feel like proof of personal failure.

Breaking Free from the Cycle

Recognizing these patterns is the first step toward change. Emotional dysregulation does not have to define you. By learning to process emotions without becoming consumed by them, interpret situations more objectively, and navigate the world with greater stability, you can break free from emotional chaos and step into a life of balance, resilience, and confidence.

This pattern influences everything—your relationships, your work, your sense of self. So take a moment. Think back to times when your emotions felt bigger than the situation warranted. When a small frustration turned into a tidal wave. When a passing comment left you spiraling.

What triggered those feelings? Were they really about the moment, or were they touching on something deeper?

Taking the First Step Toward Change

Understanding these patterns is the first step toward breaking free. This isn't about suppressing emotions or pretending they don't exist. It's about learning how to navigate them—without letting them control you.

As you explore emotional dysregulation further, you'll uncover tools to help you step out of the cycle, regain control, and approach your emotions with greater awareness and resilience. Healing is possible, and it starts with small, intentional changes. Are you ready to take that first step?

Emotional Dysregulation

Imagine Sarah, who finds herself caught in a seemingly trivial disagreement with her spouse. What begins as a simple discussion quickly escalates into a shouting match. In that moment, Sarah feels personally attacked, unable to hear her partner's constructive criticism. The emotional storm overwhelms her, and the argument spirals out of control.

Now consider Mark, who is anxiously awaiting his performance review at work. Instead of viewing the feedback as a chance to grow, his mind races with thoughts of rejection. The anxiety becomes so crippling that it clouds his judgment, making him overly sensitive to even neutral comments.

Then there's Lisa, a devoted parent who reacts with excessive anger when her child misbehaves. In the aftermath, she feels a heavy weight of shame and guilt, questioning her ability to be a good parent.

And what about Jake? Frustrated with his job, he impulsively quits without considering the consequences. Later, he grapples with regret, wishing he had taken a moment to think things through.

Finally, we meet Anna, who avoids social interactions out of fear of rejection. This fear reinforces her loneliness, creating a cycle of self-doubt and isolation.

These behaviors stem from an overactive limbic system, the part of the brain responsible for our emotional responses. When dysregulated, this system can hijack our logical thinking, making it nearly impossible to respond rationally in heated situations.

When emotions take the wheel, our ability to view situations from different angles diminishes. Conversations with loved ones become reactive rather than constructive, often resulting in chronic misunderstandings. Instead of solving problems logically, we find ourselves making impulsive decisions driven by emotion—decisions we may later regret.

Emotional dysregulation can create a tense atmosphere in relationships. Partners of individuals experiencing these struggles often feel as though they are *walking on eggshells*, fearing the next emotional outburst. Conflicts escalate quickly, leaving little room for resolution. This can lead to co-dependent dynamics, where one partner feels responsible for "fixing" the dysregulated individual, further complicating the relationship.

The Hidden Costs of Emotional Dysregulation: How It Shapes Your Self-Worth, Relationships, and Well-Being

Imagine waking up in the morning feeling confident, like you're ready to take on the world. Your energy is high, your mind is clear, and you feel like things are finally falling into place. But then, by midday, everything shifts. Maybe someone makes a critical comment at work, or you get left on the road by a friend, and suddenly, that confidence crumbles. A flood of self-doubt rushes in, washing away the positivity you felt just hours ago.

This cycle—feeling on top of the world one moment and sinking into feelings of worthlessness the next—is an all-too-common reality for those struggling with emotional dysregulation. Self-esteem becomes unstable, hinging not on personal growth or objective truth but on the intensity of ever-changing emotions. Instead of viewing mistakes as learning experiences, they become proof of deep personal failure. Instead of seeing oneself as a person with strengths and weaknesses, the mind gravitates toward extremes: *I am amazing,* or *I am worthless.*

Even the internal dialogue begins to follow this pattern. The same mind that encourages you to dream big and strive for success can, within hours, turn into your harshest critic. Thoughts like *I'm unlovable* or *I'm always going to fail* take root, creating a loop of self-doubt that is difficult to escape. Shame and guilt follow closely behind, especially after moments of emotional impulsivity—after a harsh word spoken in anger, after an emotional breakdown in public, after retreating into isolation when someone tried to help. The regret is overwhelming, yet the cycle keeps repeating.

For those experiencing emotional dysregulation, self-worth becomes fragile, dictated by external events rather than an internal sense of identity. And when self-esteem is unstable, relationships inevitably suffer.

When Emotions Control Relationships

Think about the last time you felt truly connected to someone. A friend, a partner, a family member. Now imagine that connection being overshadowed by a fear so deep it controls your every interaction—the fear of abandonment.

For many struggling with emotional dysregulation, this fear shapes how they navigate relationships. A small disagreement with a loved one can feel like a sign that the entire relationship is crumbling. A delayed text response can send them into an emotional tailspin, convincing them that they are being ignored or replaced.

This fear can manifest in two ways. Some people respond by clinging too tightly—seeking constant reassurance, needing to be reminded that they are loved and valued. The more they fear losing someone, the more they hold on, sometimes to the point of suffocation. Others go in the opposite direction—shutting down emotionally, withdrawing before anyone has the chance to hurt them. The mindset becomes: *If I don't let anyone in, they can't leave me.*

Neither approach leads to healthy, fulfilling relationships. Overdependence can strain even the strongest connections, while emotional withdrawal leads to isolation. Over time, both patterns reinforce the same core belief: *I am too much for people, or I am not enough for them.*

It's exhausting—constantly walking on eggshells, second-guessing interactions, analyzing every word, every gesture, every perceived change in tone. The weight of trying to control every outcome, to predict rejection before it happens, takes an emotional toll that leaves many feeling drained and disconnected.

And it's not just relationships with others that suffer. Emotional dysregulation impacts well-being in ways that go beyond the mind—it reaches into the body and soul.

The Toll on Well-Being: When the Mind Stays in Survival Mode

Imagine living in a house where the smoke alarm never turns off. The sound is deafening, the constant shriek making it impossible to focus, to rest, to feel safe.

This is what it's like when emotional dysregulation keeps the nervous system on high alert. The body remains in a state of chronic stress, reacting to every emotional shift as though it were a real threat. Anxiety becomes a constant companion. The mind races through worst-case scenarios, the body tenses, and exhaustion sets in.

The impact isn't just mental—it's physical. Chronic stress from emotional turmoil can lead to headaches, stomach issues, muscle tension, and even weakened immunity. The body keeps score of emotional distress, carrying the weight of every unprocessed feeling.

And then there's the spiritual disconnect. For many, faith or a sense of higher purpose brings peace and grounding. But when emotions feel uncontrollable, it can feel impossible to find stillness, to trust in something greater, to believe that healing is possible. Imagine standing at the edge of an ocean, waves crashing relentlessly, struggling to find your footing. The desire for peace is there, but it feels out of reach.

But what if it wasn't?

What if, instead of being controlled by emotions, you could learn to navigate them? What if, instead of reacting impulsively, you could pause, reflect, and respond with clarity? What if emotional dysregulation wasn't a permanent state, but something that could be understood, managed, and ultimately healed? The good news is that it can.

Reclaiming Control: Steps Toward Emotional Stability

Healing from emotional dysregulation isn't about suppressing feelings or pretending they don't exist. It's about learning how to process them without letting them take control. It's about understanding what triggers emotional spirals, recognizing the warning signs, and having tools in place to navigate them.

One of the most effective ways to regain control is through cognitive reframing—the practice of challenging and reshaping distorted thoughts. Instead of immediately believing *I always mess things up*, you learn to pause and shift perspective: *I made a mistake, but I can learn from it*. Instead of assuming *Everyone will leave me*, you replace it with: *Not everyone leaves, and I am worthy of love*.

Mindfulness practices can also help anchor emotions. Something as simple as deep breathing, grounding exercises, or meditation can create a moment of pause between impulse and reaction. The next time emotions start to surge, picture yourself pressing a pause button—taking a deep breath, feeling your feet on the ground, regaining a sense of presence before responding.

The goal isn't to ignore or suppress your emotions—but to keep them in perspective. Emotions are important; they give us valuable information about what's happening inside and around us. But when they take over completely, it becomes almost impossible to think clearly. You can't be in a calm, logical mindset and a fully reactive emotional state at the same time—it's like trying to be still and sprinting all at once. That's why staying mindful matters. Mindfulness allows you to slow down, step back, and observe your emotions without being controlled by them. It helps you engage your reasoning, so your feelings can be understood—not just reacted to.

Many men tend to go to one extreme: shutting down or denying their emotions altogether. But burying feelings doesn't make them go away; it just delays the impact. On the other hand, many women are more likely to allow emotions to take the lead, sometimes without weighing other facts or perspectives. Neither extreme is healthy. Emotional maturity means finding the middle ground—where feelings are acknowledged but not allowed to run the show.

Another powerful tool is journaling. Writing out emotions can slow down impulsive reactions, offering clarity that might not be obvious in the moment. Imagine having a space where your thoughts can flow freely, where you can track patterns, identify triggers, and begin to see progress over time.

For those who draw strength from faith, biblical reflection can provide guidance in emotional regulation. *James 1:19* reminds us to be *"quick to listen, slow to speak, and slow to become angry.*" These words encourage the practice of patience, self-awareness, and emotional control.

But most importantly, healing begins with self-compassion. Emotional dysregulation is not a personality flaw—it is a learned response, often rooted in past wounds. Recognizing this allows you to approach your struggles with understanding rather than shame. Instead of asking, *Why am I like this?* begin asking, *What can I do to heal?*

Moving Forward: Small Steps, Big Changes

True emotional stability isn't about perfection—it's about progress. It's about making small, intentional choices every day that move you toward clarity, resilience, and peace.

The next time emotions start to spiral, take a moment to pause. Breathe. Ask yourself: *Is my reaction based on the present moment, or is it tied to something deeper?* If it's the latter, remind yourself that emotions, while powerful, are not permanent. They will pass.

If you find yourself caught in negative self-talk, challenge it. Replace self-criticism with self-kindness. Speak to yourself as you would a close friend—one who is learning, growing, and healing.

And if relationships feel overwhelming, start setting small boundaries. Not walls that shut people out, but guardrails that help you navigate relationships with confidence and security.

This journey isn't easy, but it is possible. Healing is not a single moment—it is a series of choices, a process of unlearning old patterns and replacing them with new ones.

And with each step, each intentional decision, you will move closer to emotional balance, healthier relationships, and a deeper sense of self-worth.

The question is not whether change is possible. The question is: Are you ready to begin?

Chapter 2
Shaping Thoughts

Emotional dysregulation isn't just a mental struggle; it's deeply rooted in your nervous system. The way you react to stress, process emotions, and engage in relationships is largely governed by your autonomic nervous system (ANS), which has been conditioned through past experiences. When you understand how your nervous system influences your emotional responses, you can begin to see your patterns more clearly—and more importantly, learn how to change them.

Your nervous system is wired to protect you, responding to stress and perceived threats through four primary survival mechanisms: *fight*, *flight*, *freeze*, and *fawn*. These responses originate in your brain's limbic system and can override rational thought when triggered. While these mechanisms were designed to keep you safe in moments of real danger, they can also work against you when activated in everyday situations that don't actually pose a threat.

Understanding Your Survival Responses

You have a default way of responding to stress, often shaped by your early experiences. Take a moment to reflect: when faced with conflict or overwhelming emotions, how do you react?

For some, stress triggers a fight response—an instinct to confront, control, or overpower the perceived threat.

Imagine that when you receive constructive criticism at work, you immediately become defensive. You raise your voice, dismiss the feedback, and feel as if your competence is being attacked. Though you may not realize it, your nervous system is equating a simple critique with a personal threat, telling you to fight back.

Others find themselves in a flight response, where avoidance becomes the primary coping mechanism. You may notice that whenever conflict arises in your relationship, you shut down and withdraw. Rather than addressing the issue, you disengage, fearing confrontation more than the problem itself. Your nervous system has conditioned you to believe that escape is safer than facing difficult conversations.

Then there's the freeze response, where your nervous system reacts by shutting down completely. Perhaps you often find yourself unable to act when faced with unexpected pressure. Whether it's a difficult conversation, a work deadline, or a stressful event, you feel emotionally and physically paralyzed. Instead of urging you to fight or flee, your nervous system simply locks you in place, rendering you unable to respond.

Lastly, the *fawn* response leads to over-accommodation and people-pleasing as a way to avoid conflict and maintain safety. While it's less commonly recognized outside of trauma-informed settings, the fawn response is surprisingly widespread. The term was originally coined by Pete Walker[5] in his work on Complex Post-Traumatic Stress Disorder (C-PTSD), and it describes a survival strategy where individuals learn to appease others to prevent harm or emotional abandonment. You might agree with others, even against your better judgment, just to maintain peace. You find yourself saying "yes" when you want to say "no" and prioritizing others' comfort over your own needs. Your nervous system has wired you to equate approval with safety, making self-assertion feel like a risk.

Each of these responses is deeply ingrained in your body's survival instincts. They are not conscious choices, but automatic reactions designed to protect you. However, when these patterns persist beyond their usefulness, they can hinder your relationships, decision-making, and emotional well-being.

Recognizing and Shifting Your Default Response

Understanding your primary stress response is the first step toward change. Ask yourself:

- Do I react to stress with defensiveness, needing to argue or control? (Fight)
- Do I tend to avoid difficult emotions or conversations? (Flight)
- Do I freeze up, feeling unable to take action when overwhelmed? (Freeze)
- Do I over-accommodate others, neglecting my own needs to keep the peace? (Fawn)

Once you identify your go-to response, you can begin taking steps to regulate your nervous system and respond with greater awareness.

Therapeutic Self-Help Strategies for Emotional Regulation

- Recognizing Your Default Reaction – Keep a journal where you track your stress responses. Note specific situations that trigger you and how you typically react. Over time, this will help you identify patterns and recognize your responses before they take over.
- Grounding Techniques – When you feel an emotional reaction building, engage in grounding exercises such as breathwork, progressive muscle relaxation, or mindfulness. These techniques activate your parasympathetic nervous system, helping your body return to a state of calm. Check out the final chapter of this book to discover which grounding techniques are most appealing and effective for you, then practice those until they become automatic responses to emotional triggers.
- Practicing Safe Exposure – Avoidance reinforces fear. If you tend to flee or freeze in stressful situations, try gradually facing these stressors in a controlled way. For instance, if conflict makes you anxious, start by engaging in small, low-stakes disagreements where you can practice staying present and expressing yourself calmly.

By implementing these strategies, you can begin to shift your nervous system's default settings, moving from reactive survival mode to intentional, mindful responses.

As you reflect on your own patterns, consider what situations tend to activate your stress response. What strategies could you practice to bring yourself back to balance? Remember, self-awareness is the first step toward healing.

How Past Trauma Shapes Your Brain's Response to Stress

If you've ever found yourself reacting to a minor situation with overwhelming fear, sadness, or anger, you may be experiencing the effects of past trauma on your nervous system. Trauma—especially if it occurs in childhood—can rewire your brain, making it hypersensitive to perceived threats. This means that even when no real danger exists, your brain and body react as if they are under attack.

The Science Behind Trauma and Emotional Reactivity

Trauma has a profound impact on the way your brain processes information, especially when it comes to perceiving danger and responding to stress. Even long after the traumatic event has passed, your nervous system can remain in a heightened state of alert, making it difficult to differentiate between real threats and harmless situations. This happens because trauma reshapes key areas of the brain, particularly the ***amygdala, hippocampus***, and ***prefrontal cortex***—each playing a crucial role in your emotional responses, memory processing, and decision-making.

Amygdala Overactivity: Your Brain's Alarm System on High Alert

The **amygdala** is a small, almond-shaped structure deep within your brain that functions as your alarm system, detecting potential threats and initiating your fight-or-flight response. When you experience trauma, your amygdala becomes *hyperactive* and *hypersensitive*, meaning it is constantly scanning your environment for danger—even in situations where no real threat exists.

As a result, you may find yourself overreacting to minor stressors, interpreting neutral or mildly stressful events as high-risk or dangerous. This can manifest in various ways, such as:

Feeling jumpy or on edge even in safe environments

- Overreacting emotionally to situations that wouldn't normally bother you
- Experiencing panic attacks or intense fear in response to harmless triggers
- Having difficulty calming down once you feel triggered

For example, if you endured emotional abuse as a child, you may react defensively or fearfully to constructive criticism as an adult, because your amygdala interprets it as an attack rather than feedback. This overactivity of the amygdala makes it hard to distinguish between a genuine threat and a false alarm, keeping you in a heightened state of anxiety, fear, or hypervigilance.

Hippocampal Dysfunction: When the Past Feels Like the Present

The hippocampus is the part of your brain responsible for processing memories and distinguishing between past and present experiences. It plays a critical role in storing information and helping you recognize when a threat is over. However, trauma disrupts the function of the hippocampus, making it harder for you to separate old threats from new experiences.

When your hippocampus is *impaired*, you may experience:

- Flashbacks—reliving traumatic experiences as if they are happening in the present
- Intrusive memories that resurface without warning
- Exaggerated fear responses to situations that resemble past trauma
- Difficulty recalling details accurately, leading to fragmented or distorted memories

For example, if you were in a car accident, you might find yourself panicking at the sound of screeching brakes, even if you're not in immediate danger. Your hippocampus, struggling to process the difference between past and present, reactivates the fear response as if the accident were happening again. This can lead to post-traumatic stress disorder (PTSD), where past traumatic memories feel just as intense and real as they did when the event originally occurred.

A weakened hippocampus also means you may stay in a reactive state longer than necessary because your brain isn't sending clear signals that the danger has passed. Instead of processing and moving on from stressful situations, your nervous system keeps replaying the fear response, making emotional regulation extremely challenging.

Prefrontal Cortex Suppression: When Logical Thinking Shuts Down

The prefrontal cortex is the part of your brain responsible for rational thinking, impulse control, emotional regulation, and decision-making. Under normal circumstances, it helps you process emotions logically and respond to stress in a controlled way. However, when you've experienced trauma, this area becomes suppressed, meaning it doesn't function as effectively when you're under stress.

When your prefrontal cortex is *less active*, you may struggle with:

- Impulse control, making it harder to pause before reacting
- Emotional outbursts, as emotions override logical thinking
- Difficulty making decisions, feeling overwhelmed or paralyzed by choices
- Problems with self-regulation, leading to unhealthy coping mechanisms (such as avoidance, self-isolation, or substance use)

For example, if you grew up in a chaotic or abusive household, you may have learned that emotional outbursts were the only way to get your needs met. As an adult, when you face conflict, you might react impulsively with anger, withdrawal, or panic, rather than pausing to assess the situation rationally. Because trauma has weakened the prefrontal cortex, your ability to think clearly under stress is diminished, making it harder to self-regulate and respond calmly.

This suppression also explains why trauma survivors sometimes feel like they can't "think straight" in moments of distress. Their logical brain is temporarily overpowered by survival instincts, making it difficult to access reasoning and problem-solving skills when they are most needed.

The Impact of These Changes on Daily Life

The combined effects of amygdala overactivity, hippocampal dysfunction, and prefrontal cortex suppression create a cycle of emotional dysregulation that can make everyday interactions feel overwhelming.

You may:

- Overreact to small stressors without understanding why
- Struggle with memory recall or experience intrusive thoughts
- Have difficulty calming down after a triggering event
- Find decision-making and problem-solving harder in moments of stress

However, the brain is adaptable, and with the right strategies, you can begin to heal. By engaging in neuroplasticity exercises, grounding techniques, and trauma-informed therapy, you can rewire your brain to regulate emotions more effectively and break free from automatic trauma responses.

Healing takes time, but as you learn to recognize and manage these brain-based patterns, you can regain control over your emotional world—rather than being ruled by it.

For example, if you grew up in a chaotic household where expressing emotions often led to punishment, you may now find it difficult to engage in healthy emotional exchanges. Even in a loving relationship, you might lash out or withdraw when your spouse asks to have an emotional conversation. Your brain has associated vulnerability with danger, making it difficult to feel safe in these interactions.

Understanding these neurological processes can provide clarity on why certain emotional reactions feel so overwhelming—and more importantly, how to begin healing them.

Therapeutic Self-Help Strategies for Rewiring Your Brain

Trauma can leave a deep imprint on the brain, shaping how you think, feel, and respond to stress. However, the good news is that your brain has an incredible ability to change through neuroplasticity—the process of forming new neural pathways and rewiring old patterns. By engaging in intentional therapeutic exercises, you can begin to heal from past trauma and retrain your nervous system to respond in healthier, more balanced ways. Below are three powerful self-help strategies that can support your journey toward emotional regulation and healing.

1. Neuroplasticity Exercises: Rewiring Thought Patterns for Emotional Stability

Your brain is constantly adapting and evolving, meaning that even deeply ingrained trauma responses can be reshaped over time. Neuroplasticity exercises help challenge negative thought patterns that reinforce fear, anxiety, and emotional dysregulation, allowing you to replace them with healthier, more constructive ways of thinking.

One of the most effective ways to engage neuroplasticity is through cognitive reframing, which involves questioning and reshaping automatic negative thoughts. The next time you find yourself catastrophizing or assuming the worst, try the following steps:

- Pause and Identify the Thought – What is your brain telling you? Are you assuming the worst-case scenario? Are you reacting based on past trauma rather than present reality?
- Challenge the Thought – Ask yourself: Is this reaction based on actual evidence, or is it a fear-driven response? What alternative explanations might exist?
- Reframe the Thought – Replace the fearful thought with a balanced, more empowering perspective. Instead of thinking, I will fail, and everything will go wrong, reframe it to, I may struggle, but I have overcome challenges before, and I can handle this.

Another powerful neuroplasticity exercise is visualization and positive affirmations. If your brain has been conditioned to expect negative outcomes, you can counteract this by mentally rehearsing positive experiences. Imagine yourself handling stress with confidence, responding calmly to difficult situations, or navigating conflict with emotional stability. Repeating self-affirming statements like *I am safe, I am capable,* or *I can regulate my emotions* reinforces new neural pathways, making these beliefs more automatic over time.

2. Somatic Healing Techniques: Releasing Trauma Stored in the Body

Trauma is not just something you remember—it's something your body holds onto. When you experience emotional distress, your nervous system stores that tension physically, often manifesting as chronic stress, muscle tightness, or even health issues. This is why healing cannot be purely cognitive—it must also involve the body. Somatic healing techniques help discharge stored trauma and retrain your nervous system to regulate emotions more effectively.

Some of the most effective somatic healing methods include:

- Trauma-Informed Yoga – Traditional talk therapy can be helpful, but for many trauma survivors, movement-based therapies are even more effective. Trauma-informed yoga focuses on breathwork, slow movement, and grounding postures, helping you release tension and reconnect with your body in a safe way.
- Deep Breathing & Vagus Nerve Stimulation [6]– Engaging in slow, deep breathing helps activate the parasympathetic nervous system, shifting you out of

fight-or-flight mode. One simple yet powerful exercise is the 4-7-8 breathing technique: inhale for 4 seconds, hold for 7 seconds, and exhale slowly for 8 seconds.

- EMDR (Eye Movement Desensitization and Reprocessing) – This therapy is highly effective for those with PTSD, as it helps reprocess traumatic memories in a way that removes their emotional intensity. If you struggle with intrusive thoughts or flashbacks, EMDR may help you feel less triggered by past experiences.
- PMR (Progressive Muscle Relaxation). This involves systematically tensing and relaxing different muscle groups to help you become aware of where your body holds stress and then release it intentionally. Over time, incorporating daily somatic healing techniques can help regulate your nervous system, allowing you to respond to emotional triggers with greater calm and control.

3. Inner Child Work: Healing Past Emotional Wounds

Trauma often leaves an inner child longing for the comfort, reassurance, and protection that may have been missing in the past. Your inner child represents the younger version of yourself who experienced emotional wounds, and when those wounds are left unhealed, they can continue to influence your adult reactions, behaviors, and self-perception.

Inner child work helps bridge the gap between your past and present self, allowing you to nurture and comfort the parts of you that still carry fear, pain, or unmet needs. One of the most impactful exercises is writing letters to your younger self. This can be done in a journal, where you:

- Acknowledge the Pain – Write to your younger self as if you were speaking to a child in need of love and reassurance. Validate their feelings: I know you felt scared and alone, and I want you to know that wasn't your fault.
- Offer the Support You Needed – Imagine what you would say to a hurting child. Offer them the kindness, love, and encouragement they deserved, but may not have received. You are safe now. You are loved. You are strong.
- Give Yourself Permission to Heal – Let your inner child know that you, as an adult, are now capable of protecting and taking care of them. I am here for you now, and I won't let you go through this alone.

Other powerful inner child healing techniques include:

- Guided meditation – Visualizing your younger self and offering them comfort and safety.
- Speaking affirmations to yourself in the mirror – Reassuring yourself with words like You are worthy. You are enough. You are loved.
- Engaging in activities that brought you joy as a child – Art, music, nature walks, or even simple playfulness can reconnect you with a sense of security and joy.

By working with your inner child, you can **break free from old wounds**, replacing self-doubt and fear with self-compassion and empowerment.

Bringing It All Together: Integrating Healing into Daily Life

As you reflect on these strategies, consider which ones resonate with you the most. Healing is a personal journey, and different approaches work for different people. The key is consistency—even small, intentional changes can rewire your brain and nervous system over time.

Ask yourself:

- Which strategy feels most accessible to me right now?
- How can I incorporate at least one of these techniques into my daily routine?
- What reminders or cues can I use to help me stay committed to this healing process?

Healing from trauma takes time, but every step you take—whether it's reframing a negative thought, practicing a breathing technique, or offering kindness to your inner child—brings you closer to emotional freedom and resilience.

As Romans 12:2 reminds us:

> *"Do not conform to the pattern of this world, but be transformed by the renewing of your mind."*

You have the ability to *rewrite your story*, heal your mind, and reclaim your emotional well-being. Keep moving forward, one step at a time. Emotional regulation is not about suppressing emotions—it's about learning how to navigate them with awareness and intention. The more you understand your nervous system and its responses, the more empowered you become to shape your emotional world rather than be ruled by it. Each small step you take toward regulation is a step toward peace, stability, and freedom.

Chapter 3
Emotional Reactivity

The Window of Tolerance: Moving from Reactivity to Regulation.

Have you ever found yourself reacting with intense anger or panic, only to regret it later? Or perhaps you've shut down emotionally, feeling disconnected and unable to engage with those around you? These responses aren't just personality traits or bad habits—they're deeply connected to how your nervous system processes stress.

Understanding the *window of tolerance*[7] can be a game-changer for emotional regulation. This concept, rooted in neuroscience, describes the range of emotional intensity a person can handle before becoming dysregulated. When we operate within our window of tolerance, we can think clearly, engage meaningfully, and respond thoughtfully. However, when we exceed this window, we may either become overwhelmed (hyperarousal) or completely shut down (hypoarousal). Recognizing where you fall within this spectrum is the first step toward emotional balance.

How Dysregulation Manifests:

Hyperarousal: When Emotions Surge Beyond Control.

Hyperarousal occurs when emotions escalate to an unmanageable level, leading to anxiety, anger, panic, or emotional flooding. In this state, even small stressors can feel overwhelming, triggering reactions that damage relationships and leave us emotionally drained.

Take Sarah, for example. Her husband is running late, and as each minute passes, her heart pounds faster. Her mind spins through worst-case scenarios—*What if he's in an accident? What if he's avoiding me? What if something is wrong?* By the time he walks through the door, she's already consumed by fear, which quickly morphs into anger. She lashes out, accusing him of not caring, not realizing that her emotions have surged beyond her window of tolerance. Her nervous system has catapulted her into hyperarousal, where fear overrides logic and frustration replaces understanding.

Hypoarousal: When the System Shuts Down

On the other end of the spectrum, hypoarousal occurs when your nervous system shuts down in response to stress. Instead of feeling overwhelmed by emotion, you may experience emotional detachment, exhaustion, and dissociation, making it difficult to engage in meaningful interactions.

Emily knows this feeling all too well. After years of ongoing conflict in her marriage, she finds herself withdrawing completely during arguments. When her husband expresses frustration, she feels distant, her body heavy and mind foggy. She hears his words but can't bring herself to respond. Instead of reacting with anger or anxiety, her nervous system chooses disconnection as a form of self-protection. While this response may shield her from immediate emotional pain, it also prevents her from resolving issues or forming deep emotional bonds.

If you tend to shut down under stress, you might notice yourself feeling numb, fatigued, or mentally absent during difficult moments. While this may feel like a way to escape emotional discomfort, it also leaves you disengaged from life and relationships, making it harder to find connection and resolution.

Optimal Regulation: The Power of Staying Within Your Window

Now, imagine David. He and his wife are discussing a difficult subject—one that would typically escalate into an argument. But this time, David takes a deep breath. His heart beats faster, but he doesn't allow himself to be consumed by frustration. Instead of reacting defensively, he listens. He asks clarifying questions, acknowledges his wife's feelings, and expresses his own with care.

David is staying within his window of tolerance. He isn't shutting down or lashing out; he is regulating his emotions, allowing himself to remain present and connected. This ability to engage thoughtfully—even in challenging moments—is a sign of emotional resilience.

Where Do You Fall?

Think about your own experiences. Do you tend to operate in hyperarousal, feeling easily overwhelmed and reactive? Or do you lean toward hypoarousal, shutting down when emotions become too intense? Recognizing these patterns is the first step in learning to regulate them.

- Journaling Prompt: Recall a recent conflict or stressful event. How did your body and emotions react? Did you notice signs of:
  - *Hyperarousal* (racing thoughts, anger, panic)?
  - *Hypoarousal* (numbness, disconnection, avoidance)?

What might have helped you stay within your window of tolerance?

Therapeutic Strategies for Emotional Regulation

The good news? Your nervous system can be retrained. With consistent practice, you can expand your window of tolerance and learn to navigate emotions with greater ease.

1. Expanding Your Window Gradually

Like strengthening a muscle, your emotional resilience grows through gradual exposure to stress in a controlled way. If certain situations overwhelm you, start by introducing small challenges that push your limits just slightly, allowing your nervous system to adjust over time.

For example, if confrontation makes you anxious, practice voicing small concerns in non-threatening situations before tackling larger conflicts. If emotional detachment is your default response, challenge yourself to stay engaged in conversations a little longer each time before withdrawing.

These small, intentional efforts help rewire your brain, teaching it that stressful moments can be managed rather than avoided or overreacted to.

2. Co-Regulation: Finding Support in Others

The people you surround yourself with have a profound impact on your emotional regulation. Safe, supportive individuals can help stabilize your nervous system when you feel overwhelmed.

Think of a child who falls and immediately looks to a parent—if the parent reacts with panic, the child cries harder. But if the parent responds calmly and reassuringly, the child settles down more quickly. The same principle applies to adults: you regulate better in the presence of calm, emotionally stable people.

Who in your life provides that grounding presence? Consider reaching out to them during moments of distress rather than facing it alone. A simple conversation, a reassuring presence, or even a shared moment of laughter can bring you back to emotional balance.

3. Self-Regulation Techniques

When co-regulation isn't an option, self-regulation becomes essential. Engaging in sensory-based activities can help bring you back into balance when you feel emotionally dysregulated.

Try these techniques:

- **Physical Movement** – Stretching, walking, or engaging in exercise can release built-up tension and help your nervous system reset.

- **Breathwork** – Slow, intentional breathing activates the parasympathetic nervous system, calming your body. Try the 4-7-8 breathing technique: Inhale for 4 seconds, hold for 7 seconds, and exhale slowly for 8 seconds.

- **Music & Grounding Exercises** – Listening to calming music or focusing on physical sensations (like holding an object or noticing the temperature of the air) can bring you back into the present.

Next time you feel dysregulated, experiment with these techniques and note what works best for you.

4. Strengthening Your Communication Skills

Many emotional breakdowns don't happen because of the emotions themselves, but because you may lack the tools to navigate them. Learning to communicate effectively—especially when dealing with difficult people—requires practice.

Imagine you're about to have a tough conversation. Instead of bracing for battle, try preparing in advance:

- Develop key phrases that express your thoughts clearly and calmly.

- Practice setting boundaries with kindness but firmness.

- Focus on active listening, rather than just reacting.

For example, instead of immediately reacting to criticism, you might pause, take a breath, and respond with curiosity instead of defensiveness:

- *"Can you help me understand what you mean by that?"*
- *"I hear that you're frustrated. Let's talk about how we can fix this together."*

Communication is a skill, not an innate ability—and like all skills, it improves with practice.

Moving Toward Emotional Balance

Your emotional responses don't have to control you. With awareness, support, and practice, you can expand your window of tolerance, regulate emotions more effectively, and engage with life in a more meaningful, connected way. Which of these strategies feels most approachable to you? Where can you start today?

How Chronic Dysregulation Impacts Thinking and Perspective

When emotional dysregulation becomes a long-term state, it doesn't just affect your relationships—it also alters the way you think and perceive the world. Over time, living in a constant state of emotional reactivity can shape your thought patterns, making it harder to see things clearly, make rational decisions, and engage in healthy discussions.

1. Cognitive Rigidity: The Brain's Struggle with Complexity

When you are constantly in survival mode, your brain defaults to black-and-white thinking. The world begins to feel divided into extremes:

- People are either good or bad.
- Situations are either safe or dangerous.
- You either succeed or fail—there is no in-between.

This rigidity makes it difficult to see nuance, which can lead to stubbornness, misinterpretations, and ongoing conflict. Instead of allowing for complexity, your mind gravitates toward certainty, even if that certainty is based on fear rather than reality.

For example, if you've experienced betrayal in the past, you may start to believe that no one can be trusted, even when there is no real evidence of dishonesty. If you have struggled with failure, you might assume that you will always fail, causing you to avoid risks and opportunities that could lead to growth.

This kind of black-and-white thinking can make relationships, work environments, and personal growth feel like battlegrounds instead of spaces for learning and connection.

2. Confirmation Bias: Seeking What Feels Safe

When you are emotionally dysregulated, your brain seeks out information that reinforces your existing fears and assumptions. Instead of objectively analyzing situations, you may filter reality through past experiences of pain, rejection, or betrayal.

For example, if you have been deeply hurt in a relationship, you might assume dishonesty or disloyalty in others, even when there is no real evidence to support it. If you have experienced authority figures abusing power, you might distrust all leadership, believing that everyone in a position of power will eventually take advantage of you.

Take Mark, for example. He grew up in an environment where authority figures were abusive. Now, as an adult, he immediately distrusts anyone in leadership, regardless of their actual character. His past trauma prevents him from engaging in rational discussions about leadership because his brain is stuck in survival mode—always searching for confirmation that his fears are justified.

This cycle keeps you trapped, reinforcing negative assumptions instead of allowing you to see reality as it truly is.

3. Reduced Executive Functioning: The Breakdown of Logic

When stress hijacks your brain, the prefrontal cortex—the center of logic, reason, and self-regulation—goes offline. In that moment, several things happen:

- It becomes harder to engage in thoughtful discussions.
- You struggle to listen to differing opinions without becoming defensive.
- Decision-making feels overwhelming or impulsive.

In moments of emotional overwhelm, your ability to pause, analyze, and think critically disappears. Instead of responding with clarity, you might automatically:

- Jump to conclusions without considering alternative perspectives.
- React impulsively rather than engaging in problem-solving.
- Withdraw completely because thinking through complex emotions feels too exhausting.

Over time, this lack of executive functioning can lead to strained relationships, difficulty at work, and a sense of being mentally and emotionally stuck.

Strategies to Regain Intellectual Flexibility

The good news? Your brain can change. With intentional effort, you can begin rewiring your thinking patterns and expanding your ability to process emotions and information with clarity.

1. Challenge Cognitive Distortions

When you catch yourself engaging in black-and-white thinking, ask:

- Is this belief based on evidence, or am I reacting to a past wound?
- Is this an absolute truth, or is there room for nuance?
- Would I see this situation differently if I weren't feeling emotionally overwhelmed?

Before forming conclusions, challenge yourself to seek out multiple perspectives. Reality is rarely as extreme as it seems in moments of emotional distress.

2. Regulate Before Responding

If a conversation or situation triggers you, take a moment to pause before reacting.

- Breathe deeply to calm your nervous system.
- Step away momentarily if needed to prevent reactive outbursts.
- Remind yourself that responding from a place of emotional regulation leads to better outcomes than reacting impulsively.

Even a five-second pause before responding can be the difference between a conflict and a constructive conversation.

3. Practice Intellectual Curiosity

Instead of seeking validation for your existing beliefs, practice seeking understanding:

- Engage with perspectives that challenge your own rather than avoiding them.
- Ask questions rather than assuming motives.
- Read, listen, or talk to people who see the world differently—not to prove them wrong, but to expand your ability to process complexity.

The more open you become to learning, the less likely you are to get stuck in cognitive rigidity.

The Path to Emotional and Mental Clarity

Emotional regulation isn't about suppressing feelings—it's about learning to navigate them with wisdom. Expanding your window of tolerance allows you to:

- Think clearly, even in stressful situations.
- Respond thoughtfully rather than react impulsively.
- Engage in meaningful conversations without becoming defensive.
- Build relationships rooted in trust, stability, and resilience.

Healing takes time and practice, but every step you take toward regulating your emotions is a step toward mental clarity, healthier relationships, and a life of greater peace.

Take a moment to reflect on your patterns of thinking. Where in your life do you notice yourself falling into black-and-white thinking? Are there areas where you tend to see things as all good or all bad, with no in-between? Perhaps in relationships, you find yourself believing that people are either completely trustworthy or entirely unreliable. Maybe in your career, a single mistake feels like proof of failure rather than a normal part of growth. Recognizing these rigid thought patterns is the first step toward loosening their grip.

As you begin to examine your assumptions, consider how you might challenge them. Are the beliefs you hold truly based on reality, or are they shaped by past wounds or fears? When you assume the worst about a situation, is there another explanation you might be overlooking? What would it feel like to pause before reacting, to question your initial interpretations, and to allow for a more nuanced perspective? Shifting your mindset doesn't mean ignoring your instincts—it means making space for complexity, for grace, for the possibility that things aren't as extreme as they seem in moments of distress.

You don't have to overhaul your thinking overnight. Change happens in small steps, and each intentional choice you make brings you closer to emotional and intellectual balance. Perhaps today, that step is as simple as noticing when you're making an assumption and choosing to consider an alternative viewpoint. Maybe it's pausing before reacting to an emotional trigger, giving yourself a moment to breathe and recalibrate. Or it could be seeking out conversations or materials that challenge your perspective, opening yourself up to new ways of thinking.

Every effort you make moves you toward greater freedom from reactivity. Each time you slow down, challenge a rigid belief, or choose curiosity over certainty, you step closer to a life of stability, wisdom, and emotional peace.

Part 2
The Roots of Emotional Dysregulation

Chapter 4 Family Dysfunctions

Chapter 5 Betrayal Trauma

Chapter 6 Perspective Taking

Chapter 4
Family Dysfunctions

Imagine standing at the base of a mountain, gazing up at its peak. The journey ahead may seem long, and at times, the path may be steep, but with every step forward, your perspective shifts. You see new landscapes, gain strength, and find beauty in the climb itself. Emotional healing follows a similar path—it is not about reaching a fixed point but about becoming more equipped to navigate life's challenges with resilience and wisdom.

The Brain's Capacity for Lifelong Change

The science of neuroplasticity reveals that the brain has an incredible ability to adapt, rewire, and grow at any stage of life. This means that no matter how long you've struggled with emotional dysregulation, no matter how deeply ingrained certain patterns may seem, change is always possible.

- Your brain learns from repeated experiences. Just as negative thought patterns reinforce emotional instability, intentional positive habits can reshape your emotional responses.
- Healing requires practice, not perfection. The goal is not to erase pain but to learn how to respond to emotions in a way that fosters clarity and connection rather than chaos.

- Growth happens in layers. Some days you may feel like you've made great progress, while others bring old wounds to the surface. This does not mean you are failing; it means you are human.

What emotions do you often struggle with? How can you begin to validate and process those feelings today? Every small step you take in emotional regulation is a **victory worth celebrating.**

Healing Becomes a Daily Choice

Imagine waking up each morning with *a conscious decision* to nurture your emotional well-being. This is not about suppressing negative emotions or forcing positivity but about choosing to engage with your healing process in an intentional way.

For some, this may mean setting boundaries that protect their peace. For others, it may involve engaging in self-reflection, seeking professional support, or practicing mindfulness.

Consider James, who once believed his emotions controlled him. He lived in a constant state of *emotional reactivity,* feeling powerless against his anger and anxiety. But one day, he made a decision: he would start small. He committed to daily self-check-ins, mindful breathing, and structured emotional regulation exercises.

At first, it felt overwhelming, like standing on the shore of an unfamiliar ocean. But over time, he noticed something remarkable—his reactions softened, his clarity improved, and his relationships deepened. His emotions no longer dictated his actions; instead, he learned to guide them with intention.

Understanding the Roots of Emotional Dysregulation

Emotional dysregulation doesn't arise in a vacuum. It is the result of a complex interplay of early developmental disruptions, unresolved trauma, and dysfunctional relational patterns that can prevent your brain from developing healthy emotional regulation skills. Recognizing these root causes is a critical step in healing, as it allows you to understand how your past experiences shape your present reactions and relationships.

Arrested Development and Childhood Trauma

Arrested development occurs when your emotional growth is stunted due to prolonged stress, neglect, or trauma in childhood. Instead of progressing through the normal developmental stages of self-regulation, emotional intelligence, and resilience, you may find yourself emotionally stuck in a childlike state, struggling to manage emotions in a balanced and mature way.

To grasp the depth of an arrested development, it's important to first explore how your brain develops over time. The prefrontal cortex, responsible for emotional regulation and rational thought, doesn't fully mature until your mid-20s. Imagine yourself as a young child navigating a stormy sea without a life raft—if you experienced chronic stress during childhood, you may have been left adrift, unable to develop the emotional coping mechanisms needed for adulthood.

If you grew up in a volatile or unstable environment, you likely learned to react to stress with survival instincts rather than self-soothing techniques. For example, when faced with conflict or criticism, your instinct may be to flee, shut down, or lash out, much like a frightened animal. These emotional reactions, which were once necessary for self-protection, can persist in adulthood, showing up as impulsivity, emotional outbursts, or dependency on others for validation and stability. You may find yourself struggling with emotions that feel too intense, too unpredictable, or too overwhelming, making it difficult to feel in control of your responses.

If you recognize these patterns in yourself, know that you are not alone. Emotional dysregulation is not a personal failing—it is often a learned response to early experiences of stress or instability. The good news is that your brain is capable of change, and with the right tools and awareness, you can develop the emotional regulation skills that may have been missing in your early years. Healing begins with understanding where these patterns come from, and from there, you can start to rewrite your emotional responses, creating a more balanced and secure future.

Let's consider Sarah, for example. At 35, she panics and shuts down whenever she is criticized at work. Despite being a competent professional, her reactions are steeped in fear and avoidance—echoing her childhood response to her father's unpredictable anger. Sarah's story serves as a poignant reminder of how unresolved childhood traumas can shape adult behaviors.

Recognizing the patterns of emotional dysregulation is like finally turning on the lights in a dark room. For so long, you may have stumbled through life, reacting without fully understanding why certain situations triggered such intense responses. But now, as you begin to see these patterns clearly, you have the power to change them. Healing doesn't happen all at once—it's a process of learning new ways to care for yourself, to respond to emotions with wisdom rather than impulse, and to rebuild the parts of you that have long been neglected.

One of the most profound ways to begin this process is through inner child work—an exercise in self-compassion that allows you to connect with the younger version of yourself, the part of you that still carries the pain of unmet needs and past wounds. Imagine sitting down and writing a letter to your younger self, speaking to them with the kindness and understanding they may not have received at the time. What would you say? Would you remind them that they were worthy of love, even when they felt unseen? Would you comfort them in the moments they felt abandoned or unheard? This practice isn't about changing the past—it's about acknowledging it, validating the emotions that were never given space to be felt, and offering the nurturing that was missing.

The Power of the Narrative

Another powerful tool in your healing journey is **journaling emotional triggers**. Throughout the day, there are moments when your reaction feels far bigger than the situation itself—when a critical comment from a coworker leaves you feeling deeply ashamed, or when a friend cancels plans makes you feel unexpectedly abandoned. These moments often aren't just about the present situation; they are echoes of past experiences, resurfacing in the now. By keeping a journal of these triggers, you begin to notice patterns. What situations consistently bring out childlike reactions—defensiveness, withdrawal, intense fear of rejection? Writing them down gives you the ability to step back and examine them with curiosity rather than judgment. It's the first step in replacing automatic reactions with thoughtful, intentional responses.

As you become more aware of these patterns, the next step is learning how to develop adult coping strategies—the tools that will allow you to navigate emotions with greater resilience and self-awareness. Instead of reacting impulsively, you practice self-talk, reminding yourself that your feelings, while valid, do not have to control you. Instead of allowing fear of abandonment to dictate your relationships, you learn to set healthy boundaries that protect both your needs and your connections with others. Instead of being consumed by emotional distress, you ground yourself in the present, using breathing exercises or mindfulness techniques to bring yourself back to reality.

Healing is not about never feeling triggered again—it's about learning how to handle those triggers differently. It's about recognizing that while your emotions may be rooted in the past, your responses belong to the present. Through inner child work, journaling, and developing healthier coping mechanisms, you begin to rewrite the way you experience emotions, replacing old wounds with new wisdom.

This process takes time, but every small step is a step toward freedom—toward a life where emotions no longer control you, but instead, guide you toward deeper understanding and growth—to start listening to yourself in a new way?

As you embark on this journey of self-discovery and growth, reflect on the words from 1 Corinthians 13:11: "When I was a child, I spoke like a child, I thought like a child, I reasoned like a child. When I became a man, I gave up childish ways." This passage serves as a powerful reminder that both spiritual and emotional maturity require intentional effort to transcend past wounds.

Breaking Free from Family Dysfunction:

Jason grew up in a home where emotions were treated as weaknesses. If he cried, he was mocked. If he expressed frustration, he was told to "get over it." If he showed vulnerability, he was made to feel ashamed. The message was clear: emotions were not welcome here. Over time, Jason learned to keep his feelings locked away, convinced that silence was safer than expression.

But the cost of that silence was high. As he moved into adulthood, he found himself caught in a cycle he couldn't escape. Whenever something upset him, he either bottled it up until he erupted in anger, or he avoided difficult conversations entirely, fearing the discomfort of emotional exposure. Relationships felt distant, his frustrations simmered beneath the surface, and despite his best efforts to push through life unaffected, he couldn't shake the feeling that something was missing.

Like Jason, many who grow up in dysfunctional family environments develop maladaptive coping mechanisms—patterns of behavior that helped them survive in childhood but now hinder them in adulthood. Some become overly enmeshed in relationships, lacking boundaries and fearing independence. Others, like Jason, learn to shut down, emotionally disconnecting to avoid the risk of rejection or ridicule. Whether the dysfunction stemmed from neglect, control, or inconsistency, the result is the same: difficulty processing emotions in a healthy way.

For Jason, breaking free from these ingrained patterns meant first identifying family patterns—recognizing the messages he had absorbed about emotions and how they still influenced his responses. He took time to reflect on his past, asking himself, *What did I learn about expressing emotions? What was I told about anger, sadness, or fear?* The answers revealed how deeply his childhood had shaped his emotional struggles.

But awareness alone wasn't enough. Jason needed to relearn emotional expression—to practice communicating his feelings in ways that felt authentic but safe. At first, it felt unnatural, like speaking a language he had never been taught. But little by little, he experimented with expressing himself—not through outbursts or avoidance, but through assertive communication. He learned to say things like, *"That hurt me,"* or *"I need some space right now,"* instead of withdrawing in silence or reacting with anger.

Most importantly, Jason found healing through safe relationships. He sought out friends who listened without judgment, who encouraged his growth rather than dismissing his feelings. In these relationships, he discovered something unfamiliar but life-changing: emotional safety. Slowly, he began to trust that expressing his emotions wouldn't lead to rejection but to deeper connection.

If you've ever felt like Jason—trapped by emotional patterns you didn't choose but can't seem to escape—know that change is possible. By recognizing how your past has shaped your present, practicing healthy emotional expression, and surrounding yourself with safe, supportive people, you can begin to rewrite your emotional story. It won't happen overnight, but each small step is a move toward freedom.

Now, take a moment to reflect: What messages did you receive about emotions growing up? What patterns have you carried into adulthood that no longer serve you? Change begins with awareness, but transformation happens when you take intentional steps toward healing.

The Lingering Impact of Abandonment: Finding Security After a Painful Past

For many, the wounds of early abandonment don't just fade with time. They linger, shaping the way they see themselves, others, and the world around them. Trust feels fragile, relationships feel unpredictable, and even in moments of security, there's a gnawing fear that it could all be taken away.

These wounds often stem from childhood experiences—whether it was growing up in foster care, being raised by emotionally unavailable parents, or experiencing deep loss at a young age. The pain of not feeling securely attached creates hypervigilance—an ever-present anxiety that people will leave, that love is conditional, that safety is temporary. This emotional imprint doesn't just affect how someone feels; it affects how they relate to others.

For some, it manifests as anxious attachment—a desperate need for reassurance, an over-reliance on partners or friends to feel whole. For others, it appears as avoidant attachment—an instinct to push people away before they get too close, to maintain control by never allowing deep emotional connections. And for those caught in between, disorganized attachment creates an unpredictable pattern of craving intimacy while fearing it at the same time.

Understanding these attachment styles was the first step toward healing for Maya, who had spent most of her life believing she was unlovable. She had been in and out of foster homes as a child, each transition reinforcing the idea that relationships were fleeting, that she was disposable. As an adult, she found herself sabotaging relationships—either clinging too tightly or leaving before she could be left.

Her journey toward healing began with understanding attachment styles—recognizing how her childhood experiences had wired her to react to intimacy and trust. For the first time, she saw that her fear of abandonment wasn't a personality flaw; it was a learned survival response. And because it was learned, it could also be unlearned.

Maya then began the process of reparenting herself—giving herself the love, security, and validation she had never received as a child. Instead of looking to others to fill the void, she practiced self-compassion. She spoke to herself the way a loving parent would: *You are worthy. You are enough. You don't have to earn love.*

But true healing happened when she started developing secure attachments—intentionally building relationships with people who were consistent, trustworthy, and safe. It wasn't easy; at times, she still felt the urge to withdraw or seek excessive reassurance. But over time, she learned to trust in something she had never believed possible: stability.

If you've ever struggled with abandonment wounds, know that they do not have to define you. Your past may have shaped your fears, but it does not have to control your future. You can learn to trust, to build healthy relationships, to feel secure within yourself.

Take a moment to reflect: How has your past shaped the way you approach relationships today? What steps can you take to nurture yourself and build trust in safe relationships?

Chapter 5
Betrayal Trauma

Understanding Betrayal Trauma: The Emotional Fallout of Broken Trust

Now, let's delve into another layer of emotional complexity: betrayal trauma. This form of trauma occurs when you experience profound emotional damage from a violation of trust, often from someone close to you—a spouse, parent, mentor, or friend. When trust is shattered, it can disrupt your nervous system, leading to heightened emotional reactivity, deep insecurity, and a persistent sense of unease in relationships.

When betrayal occurs, your brain's amygdala—the center responsible for fear—becomes hyperactive. Imagine walking alone through a dark alley, always on edge, perceiving every shadow as a potential threat. Your nervous system becomes primed for danger, making it difficult to feel safe in future relationships. Even in moments of security, you may find yourself waiting for the other shoe to drop, constantly scanning for signs of deception or abandonment.

Betrayal trauma often creates an emotional rollercoaster, where you swing between trust and suspicion. You may desperately want to believe in the goodness of others, yet at the same time, fear getting hurt again. It's common to internalize the betrayal, questioning whether it happened because of some personal flaw or inadequacy. This internal struggle can fuel shame, depression, and anxiety, leaving you feeling unworthy of love and connection.

If you have experienced betrayal trauma, know that your reactions are not irrational—they are the result of your brain and body trying to protect you from further harm. But healing is possible. As you begin to acknowledge and process these wounds, you can work toward restoring your sense of trust—not just in others, but in yourself. By addressing the pain of betrayal, you create space for emotional clarity, self-worth, and healthier relationships moving forward.

Learning to Heal and Trust Again

Mark never thought his marriage would end this way. After ten years of partnership, shared dreams, and the quiet comfort of a life built together, he discovered his wife had been unfaithful. The betrayal hit like a tidal wave, pulling him under, leaving him gasping for air in an emotional storm he never saw coming. One moment, he was consumed by rage, his mind replaying every lie, every deception. The next, an unbearable sadness settled over him, numbing him to the world around him. And then there were times when he felt nothing at all—just a hollow detachment, as if his heart had shut down entirely to avoid the pain.

Each day became a battle. Even in ordinary conversations, his wounds resurfaced. A harmless disagreement with a friend could send him spiraling, convinced that trust was an illusion, that betrayal was always just around the corner.

The emotional rollercoaster left him exhausted and disoriented, unsure of how to rebuild his life when everything he had known felt like a lie.

Mark's journey toward healing was not instant, nor was it easy. But as he began to search for ways to make sense of his pain, he discovered strategies that helped him process his emotions, regain control, and slowly, cautiously, open himself to trust again.

One of the most powerful tools he encountered was *narrative therapy*—the practice of writing down his experience, not just as a list of painful events, but as a story with depth and meaning. At first, it was overwhelming. The words felt too raw, too real. But as he continued, something shifted. He began to see the betrayal not as a reflection of his worth, but as something separate from himself. By putting pen to paper, he could untangle his identity from what had happened to him. He was not just "the man who was betrayed." He was more than his pain. He was someone still capable of healing, of growth, of love.

But even as his understanding of the past deepened, the question of trust remained. *How do you trust again when trust has been shattered?* Mark knew he couldn't just force himself to believe in people overnight. So instead, he started small. He let safe relationships prove themselves—not through grand promises, but through consistent, reliable actions. He paid attention to the people who showed up, who honored their word, who demonstrated that trustworthiness wasn't just something spoken, but something lived. Slowly, the walls he had built began to lower, not all at once, but piece by piece.

Healing, however, requires more than just processing emotions and rebuilding trust. Mark had to regain control over his own nervous system, which had been hijacked by the trauma of betrayal. The smallest triggers could send his heart racing, his thoughts spiraling into worst-case scenarios.

To regain a sense of calm, he began practicing *mindfulness and emotional regulation exercises*—small but powerful habits that helped him find steadiness in the chaos. Some days, it was as simple as focusing on his breath, inhaling for four counts, holding for four, exhaling for four—a technique known as box breathing. Other days, he turned to progressive muscle relaxation, releasing the tension he hadn't even realized he was carrying. And in moments of overwhelming sadness, he found solace in prayerful meditation, reminding himself that even when trust in people felt fragile, there was a deeper foundation he could lean on.

Mark's journey was not about erasing the past or pretending the betrayal never happened. It was about learning to live with it in a way that no longer controlled him. It was about reclaiming his identity, his ability to trust, and his capacity for peace.

If you, like Mark, have faced betrayal, know that healing is possible. The road forward may feel uncertain, but step by step, with intentionality and grace, you can rebuild. The pain may be part of your story, but it does not have to be the whole story. You are more than what has been done to you. You are still capable of trust, of hope, of a future that is not defined by your past.

In moments of deep pain, you can turn to the wisdom found in scripture: *"The Lord is close to the brokenhearted and saves those who are crushed in* spirit" (Psalm 34:18). This verse reminds you that healing from betrayal begins by opening your hearts to God's love, which can restore broken trust.

Take a moment to journal your feelings surrounding betrayal and consider small steps toward rebuilding trust in your relationships.

Choosing Healing: The First Step Toward Emotional Freedom

The road to emotional regulation isn't a straight path. It's a journey filled with reflection, intentional action, and patience. Emotional dysregulation—whether it stems from childhood wounds, betrayal, or family dysfunction—can feel overwhelming, but it is not a life sentence.

Healing begins with awareness. It starts when you look at the patterns that no longer serve you and choose to break them. It grows when you practice new ways of expressing emotions, building trust, and fostering inner security. And it is sustained through daily commitment—whether through self-help strategies, therapy, or spiritual reflection.

Right now, you have a choice. You can continue operating in the emotional cycles that keep you stuck, or you can take a step toward healing. It doesn't have to be a grand gesture—sometimes, healing begins with something as small as writing down a thought, expressing a feeling, or setting a boundary.

So, what will your first step be? Will you reflect on the messages you received about emotions? Will you practice self-compassion instead of self-criticism? Will you allow yourself to trust—just a little—knowing that healing happens one step at a time?

No matter where you are on this journey, remember this: You are not broken. You are not beyond repair. Healing is possible, and it begins the moment you choose it.

Chapter 6
Perspective Taking

How Emotional Dysregulation Distorts Relationships and Reality

Emotional dysregulation doesn't just influence your internal world—it completely reshapes how you interact with others and how you interpret reality. Imagine a scenario where a small disagreement with a loved one unexpectedly escalates into a full-blown emotional crisis. A single comment, one that wasn't meant to be hurtful, suddenly feels like a personal attack. The rational part of your brain understands that the situation is minor, yet your emotions tell a different story, fueling anger, panic, or deep sadness.

This is the daily struggle of emotional dysregulation. It creates a world where emotions override logic, leading to impulsive reactions, strained relationships, and a constant sense of instability. When you struggle with emotional regulation, even neutral situations can feel threatening, causing misunderstandings that quickly spiral into conflict. Your perception of reality becomes distorted, shaped not by what is actually happening, but by the intensity of your emotional responses. This can make it difficult to maintain trust, build healthy relationships, or feel secure in your connections with others.

Recognizing these patterns is the first step toward breaking free from them. By understanding how emotional dysregulation manifests in relationships, you can begin to shift toward healthier, more stable interactions. Let's explore some of the most common ways this pattern plays out and how you can start reclaiming control over your emotional world.

The Push-Pull Dynamic: The Cycle of Craving Closeness but Fearing Intimacy

One of the most painful relational patterns that emotional dysregulation creates is the push-pull dynamic—a cycle of seeking closeness only to withdraw the moment it's offered. This back-and-forth dance is driven by two opposing fears: the fear of abandonment and the fear of engulfment. On one hand, there's a deep, almost desperate need for connection; on the other, an equally intense fear of being controlled, rejected, or hurt.

Sarah knows this pattern all too well. When she starts dating someone new, she craves their attention, texting often, planning outings, and seeking reassurance that they truly care. But as soon as her partner starts reciprocating, she feels overwhelmed. Thoughts creep in: *What if this is too much? What if they see the real me and decide I'm not enough?* Fear overrides her initial excitement, and suddenly, she pulls away—canceling plans, taking longer to respond to messages, or finding reasons why the relationship won't work.

This leaves her partner confused, caught in the cycle of being pulled in and pushed away, never quite sure where they stand. The more Sarah avoids intimacy, the lonelier she feels, and the cycle continues.

Psychological Explanation:

- The fear of abandonment triggers a deep craving for connection.
- The fear of engulfment or rejection prompts withdrawal when intimacy is within reach.
- This creates an unstable relationship pattern where emotional needs are never fully met.

Healing the Push-Pull Dynamic

If you find yourself stuck in this pattern, awareness is the first step to change. Keeping a journal can help track moments when you feel the urge to pull away or desperately cling to someone. Pay attention to the emotions that arise and ask yourself: *What am I actually afraid of?* Learning to tolerate emotional closeness—without withdrawing or overwhelming your partner—takes practice. Seeking therapy, particularly attachment-focused approaches, can help develop more secure relational patterns. Building self-trust is key; the more you learn to regulate your own emotions, the less dependent you become on external validation to feel secure.

The Fear of Abandonment: When Anxiety Takes Over

For many people with emotional dysregulation, the fear of abandonment is ever-present. Even in stable relationships, the anxiety of being left behind lurks beneath the surface, causing hypersensitivity to signs of rejection. A delayed text response, a canceled plan, or a shift in a loved one's tone can trigger overwhelming panic.

Mike experiences this fear daily. He checks his partner's phone obsessively, searching for any sign that she might be losing interest. When she's busy and doesn't respond right away, his mind spirals: *Is she ignoring me? Is she tired of me?* His heart pounds, his hands shake, and before he can stop himself, he's sending multiple messages, demanding reassurance. His partner, feeling smothered, pulls away slightly, which only intensifies Mike's fear.

What Mike doesn't realize is that his brain has been wired to expect abandonment. His past experiences—whether childhood neglect, unstable relationships, or unresolved trauma—have trained his nervous system to view even small separations as threats. His amygdala, the brain's fear center, remains on high alert, scanning for danger where there may be none. This overactive fear response creates a self-fulfilling prophecy: the more he seeks control, the more distance his partner needs, reinforcing his deepest fear of being left alone.

Healing from the Fear of Abandonment

Breaking free from this cycle starts with challenging old narratives. Just because someone in the past abandoned you doesn't mean every person in your life will. Practicing grounding techniques, such as deep breathing or progressive muscle relaxation, can help soothe the nervous system when abandonment anxiety strikes. Learning to tolerate small separations—like spending an afternoon apart without checking in—can build emotional resilience.

Most importantly, reframing negative thoughts by asking, *What is the evidence that I'm being abandoned?* helps distinguish between past fears and present reality.

Emotional Explosions: When Small Conflicts Become Major Battles

For some, emotional dysregulation takes the form of explosive reactions. A minor frustration can quickly escalate into yelling, accusations, or impulsive actions that later lead to regret.

Lisa struggles with this daily. One evening, her husband forgets to call after work. Instead of brushing it off or calmly addressing it, Lisa's emotions spiral out of control. *If he loved me, he would have called. He doesn't care.* Before she knows it, she's sending angry messages, accusing him of neglect, fueling an argument that leaves both of them feeling hurt and disconnected.

In reality, Lisa's emotional brain is hijacking her rational thinking. When stress arises, the prefrontal cortex, responsible for logical reasoning, shuts down, allowing the emotional centers of the brain to take over. In this state, the brain misinterprets neutral situations as threats, turning small incidents into overwhelming crises.

Breaking the Pattern of Explosive Reactions

The first step toward change is learning to pause before reacting. When an emotional trigger hits, take a deep breath and give yourself space. Implement a "delayed response" rule, stepping away for five minutes before saying anything. Practicing cognitive reframing—challenging catastrophic thoughts by asking, *Is this actually true, or am I reacting from fear?*—helps prevent unnecessary escalation. Writing emotions down before expressing them aloud can also be incredibly effective. By processing feelings privately first, you can communicate in a way that fosters connection rather than conflict.

Moving Toward Emotional Balance

If any of these patterns resonate with you, take a moment to remind yourself of this essential truth: healing is possible. Emotional dysregulation is not a fixed condition; it is a learned response, shaped by past experiences, and—most importantly—it can be rewired with intentional effort and practice.

This journey begins with small but powerful choices. The next time an overwhelming emotion surges within you, pause. Take a deep breath. Instead of reacting impulsively, give yourself space to observe your thoughts and feelings before taking action. Challenge fearful thoughts by asking yourself whether they are based on present reality or past wounds. Work toward emotional consistency by practicing self-soothing techniques and recognizing that feelings, while valid, are not always accurate reflections of truth.

You are not your past. You are not your emotions. You are the person who is learning to cope with and deal with your past and your emotions. And you have the power to heal, to grow, and to create relationships built on trust, stability, and genuine connection. The road to emotional balance requires courage, patience, and self-compassion, but every step forward is a step toward freedom. You are capable of walking this path, and you are not alone.

How Past Trauma Distorts Present Interactions

Have you ever found yourself overreacting to a situation, only to realize later that your response was out of proportion? Maybe your partner forgot to text you back, and suddenly you felt a wave of panic convinced they were losing interest in you. Or perhaps a coworker offered constructive criticism, and instead of seeing it as helpful feedback, you felt humiliated and inadequate. These responses may seem irrational in the moment, but they often stem from unhealed trauma that distorts the way we interpret present interactions.

The human brain is wired for survival, and past trauma can rewire it to anticipate danger even where none exists. When unresolved pain lingers beneath the surface, everyday situations can feel like threats. The brain, trained by past wounds, reacts defensively to protect itself, even when no real harm is present.

Consider Anna's experience. After enduring an abusive relationship, she entered a new partnership with someone kind and emotionally available. Yet, the first time her new boyfriend raised his voice slightly—without anger, just in the course of an animated conversation—her body flooded with fear. Her mind immediately went to worst-case scenarios: *He's going to hurt me. I need to leave before things get worse.* Despite her partner having no history of mistreating her, Anna's past trauma had conditioned her brain to associate raised voices with danger. She was not responding to the present moment; she was reacting to the past.

Recognizing when past wounds shape present interactions is a crucial step toward healing.

Here are some strategies to help navigate this process:

1. Identifying Trauma Triggers: The first step is awareness. Pay attention to situations that evoke strong emotional reactions. Ask yourself, *Is this situation truly dangerous, or am I responding to an old wound?* Keeping a journal of triggering moments can help identify recurring patterns and provide insight into which past experiences might still be affecting you.

2. Practicing Reality Testing: When emotions flare up, pause and ask yourself, *Is my current reaction proportionate to the situation?* If a friend cancels plans, does it really mean they don't care about you, or is it possible they're simply busy? When your partner is quiet, does it mean they're angry at you, or could they just be tired? Learning to differentiate between real threats and perceived ones is a vital part of emotional regulation.

3. Seeking Professional Support: Therapy can provide a structured and supportive space to process past trauma and learn new coping mechanisms. Modalities such as cognitive-behavioral therapy (CBT), eye movement desensitization and reprocessing (EMDR), and somatic therapy can help rewire the brain's response to perceived threats.

Healing from trauma takes time, but every step toward self-awareness moves you closer to emotional freedom. As you work through these strategies, reflect on how past experiences may influence your present reactions. With patience and persistence, you can learn to distinguish between real and perceived threats, allowing you to engage with the world more rationally and peacefully.

Why Disagreement Feels Like a Personal Attack

Imagine sitting in a conversation where someone expresses a viewpoint that starkly contrasts your own. Your heart begins to race, your palms grow sweaty, and suddenly, you feel defensive—almost as if your identity itself is under attack. Rather than engaging in a calm discussion, you might find yourself shutting down, lashing out, or feeling personally wounded by the difference in perspective. This isn't just a random reaction; it's a reflection of how emotional dysregulation can shape the way we handle disagreement.

Many people who struggle with emotional regulation find it difficult to separate their opinions from their sense of self-worth. When confronted with an opposing view, the mind misinterprets the disagreement as rejection. This reaction often stems from early experiences of conditional love or attachment wounds, where approval and acceptance were tied to compliance rather than individuality.

The brain, always seeking safety, treats disagreement as a potential threat. This is especially true for those with insecure attachment styles, where differing opinions may trigger fears of abandonment. Emotional reasoning—where feelings dictate perceived reality—takes control, making it nearly impossible to engage in logical analysis. A simple difference of opinion can feel like a direct assault on one's value as a person.

To develop a healthier relationship with disagreement, consider these strategies:

1. Practicing Intellectual Humility: Remind yourself that differing viewpoints do not equate to personal rejection. Being open to new perspectives doesn't mean abandoning your own beliefs; it simply means recognizing that multiple viewpoints can exist without diminishing your worth.

2. Separating Emotion from Argument: When faced with an opposing opinion, pause and ask yourself, *Am I reacting emotionally, or am I engaging with the argument itself?* Learning to distinguish between feelings and facts can prevent unnecessary emotional distress.

3. Strengthening a Secure Self-Identity: Work on developing self-worth that isn't reliant on external validation. When your confidence is rooted in who you are rather than what others think, disagreement becomes far less threatening.

Think back to a time when a disagreement felt like a personal attack. What was it about that moment that made it feel so charged? By reflecting on these experiences and practicing emotional regulation, you can learn to engage in discussions without feeling overwhelmed by emotion.

Rewiring Emotional Responses: The Path to Healing and Stability

Emotional dysregulation can distort the way you perceive reality and relationships, fueling push-pull dynamics, abandonment fears, and emotional explosions. When emotions run unchecked, they can create patterns of instability that leave you feeling exhausted, misunderstood, and disconnected. But the good news is that these patterns are not permanent. Healing begins with awareness—recognizing when your reactions are rooted in past experiences rather than present reality.

Through mindfulness, reality testing, and self-compassion, you can begin to rewire your emotional responses, creating space for healthier interactions. Instead of reacting impulsively, you can learn to pause, reframe, and respond with clarity. By practicing self-regulation, seeking professional guidance, and committing to intentional self-growth, you set the foundation for greater relational stability and emotional clarity.

Every small effort matters. Each time you take a breath before reacting, challenge a fearful thought, or choose patience over impulsivity, you reinforce new neural pathways that lead to emotional balance. It's a process—one that requires time and persistence—but it is entirely within your reach.

As you move forward, take a moment to reflect on the areas where emotional dysregulation has impacted your life. Where do you notice patterns of reactivity, fear, or avoidance? What small steps can you take today to shift toward greater emotional stability?

Your emotions do not define you. You have the power to change, to heal, and to build relationships that are grounded in trust, security, and understanding. The journey may not always be easy, but it is absolutely worth it. And the first step begins now.

Part 3
Healing Emotional Dysregulation

Chapter 7 Emotional Awareness

Chapter 8 Finding Calm Within

Chapter 9 Healing Betrayal

Chapter 10 Building Resilience

Chapter 7
Emotional Awareness

Breaking the Cycle: Developing Emotional Awareness

Healing from emotional dysregulation begins with a single, foundational step: awareness. Before you can manage your emotions effectively, you must first understand them—where they come from, how they influence your thoughts and actions, and how past experiences shape your responses to the present. Without this understanding, you may remain trapped in reactive cycles, reliving old wounds in new situations. But when you cultivate emotional awareness, you begin to take back control.

Emotional awareness allows you to shift from unconscious reaction to conscious response. It enables you to recognize when you are being triggered, to pause before reacting impulsively, and to separate past wounds from present reality. The path to emotional regulation is not about suppressing emotions but about understanding them—learning their patterns, their roots, and navigating them with wisdom.

This chapter explores the power of emotional awareness and provides practical strategies for cultivating a more intentional and balanced emotional life.

Identifying Personal Triggers: When the Past Hijacks the Present

Have you ever found yourself having an emotional reaction that seemed far stronger than the situation warranted? Perhaps someone made an offhand comment, and suddenly, you felt an intense wave of anger, hurt, or shame. Logically, you knew their words weren't meant to wound you, yet the feeling was overwhelming.

This is the power of emotional triggers—situations, words, actions, or even memories that provoke intense emotional responses, often tied to past wounds rather than the present moment.

The Science of Emotional Triggers

Your brain is wired to protect you. Deep within its structures, the amygdala—often called the brain's fear center—acts as a security system, constantly scanning for danger. When it detects something that resembles a past painful experience, it sends out distress signals before the rational part of your brain even has time to assess the situation. This can cause you to react with heightened emotions, even when no real threat exists.

Think of a child who was frequently ignored or dismissed by their caregivers. As an adult, they may interpret their partner's need for personal space as rejection. The logical mind might recognize that their partner simply needs a quiet moment, but the emotional brain relives the childhood fear of abandonment, leading to anxiety, anger, or withdrawal.

Take Alex, for example. He grew up with an emotionally distant father who rarely acknowledged his feelings. Now, as an adult, whenever his wife seems distracted or preoccupied, he spirals into panic and resentment. He assumes she is losing interest, though in reality, she is simply thinking about work. His reaction—becoming clingy, demanding reassurance, or starting an argument—stems from past wounds rather than the reality of the present moment.

Understanding these triggers is the first step toward breaking free from their control. When you recognize that your emotional response is tied to the past, you can begin to separate old pain from current reality, allowing you to respond with clarity rather than reactivity.

Recognizing Your Triggers

To begin healing, you must first identify your triggers. Pay attention to moments when your emotions feel out of proportion to the situation. Keep a journal to record these experiences, noting what happened, how you felt, and any patterns that emerge.

- What situations provoke the strongest emotional reactions in you?
- Are there recurring themes—rejection, criticism, control, abandonment?
- Do these reactions mirror experiences from your past?

By tracking these moments, you can start to recognize when old wounds are resurfacing and begin to separate past pain from present reality.

Shifting Your Perspective

When you feel triggered, pause and ask yourself:

"Is this situation truly the same as my past experience, or does it just feel similar?"

This simple question creates space for reflection and prevents past emotions from hijacking the present. Instead of reacting impulsively, you can step back and assess the situation with clarity.

Learning to Pause Before Reacting: The Power of the Pause

Emotional reactivity often stems from acting on impulse rather than intention. When we react without pausing, we risk saying things we don't mean, making decisions we later regret, and deepening relational wounds. But when we master the art of pausing, we create an opportunity to choose our response rather than be ruled by emotion.

Imagine a moment when a friend makes a remark that stings. Your instinct is to snap back, to defend yourself. But what if, instead, you took a deep breath? That small pause could be the difference between an emotional outburst and a thoughtful response.

The Neuroscience of Reactivity

When emotions run high, the brain's fight-or-flight system takes over, overriding the rational prefrontal cortex. This is why, in moments of stress, we often say or do things we later regret. Learning to pause interrupts this process, allowing our logical brain to reengage before we act.

The 90-Second Rule: Taking Back Control

Neuroscientist Jill Bolte Taylor[8] discovered that emotional reactions typically last about 90 seconds. If we can pause and breathe through those initial moments, we reclaim the power to choose our response rather than react impulsively.

Take Jessica, for instance. Her boss criticizes her work, and her immediate reaction is to lash out or quit on the spot. But instead of succumbing to that impulse, she takes a deep breath and gives herself time to process the feedback. By the time she responds, she has calmed her emotions and can engage in a constructive conversation rather than an emotional explosion.

Differentiating Between Past Wounds and Present Experiences

Unhealed trauma has a way of distorting the present. When we carry unresolved pain, we may find ourselves reacting to current situations as if they were past threats. This phenomenon, sometimes called *emotional time travel,* causes our brains to respond to present circumstances with the intensity of past wounds.

How Trauma Distorts Perception

- Trauma Encoding: The brain encodes painful memories in a fragmented way, making them feel immediate and overwhelming, even years later.
- Projection: Unresolved wounds can lead us to project past fears onto present relationships, causing misunderstandings and unnecessary conflict.

Consider Michael, who was abandoned by his mother as a child. As an adult, when his wife asks for space after a long day, he interprets her silence as rejection. His emotional brain relives the fear of abandonment, triggering a response that is disproportionate to the situation.

Healing Through Awareness

To break free from this pattern, ask yourself:

"What actual evidence do I have that this situation is the same as my past, or does it just feel that way?"

By consciously separating past pain from present reality, you can prevent old wounds from distorting your relationships.

Applying These Lessons

Healing from emotional dysregulation is a journey—one that begins with self-awareness. By recognizing your triggers, practicing the power of the pause, and differentiating between past wounds and present experiences, you take back control of your emotional landscape.

Remember, every moment of awareness is a step toward healing. The next time you feel overwhelmed by emotion—pause. Breathe. Reflect. Choose your response with intention. Over time, these small shifts will lead to profound transformation, allowing you to engage with life from a place of clarity, strength, and emotional balance.

Your past does not have to dictate your future. With awareness and intentional practice, you can break the cycle and cultivate the emotional resilience needed to build a life of deeper connection, peace, and personal empowerment.

Chapter 8
Finding Calm Within

Developing Self-Soothing Practices: Learning to Find Calm Within

Emotions can often feel like waves crashing against the shore—sometimes gentle, sometimes overwhelming. If you struggle with emotional dysregulation, the ability to self-soothe may seem out of reach. Instead of finding peace within, you might rely on external sources to escape uncomfortable feelings—substance use, avoidance, aggression, or distraction. But true emotional resilience comes from learning how to regulate emotions in healthy ways, without depending on external validation or temporary fixes.

Self-soothing is the practice of calming yourself in moments of distress, using intentional techniques that activate your brain's natural relaxation response. By developing these skills, you can shift from reactive, impulsive coping mechanisms to proactive emotional regulation, building a foundation for long-term emotional stability.

The Science Behind Self-Soothing: Why It Works

At its core, self-soothing isn't just about feeling better in the moment—it's about rewiring your brain for long-term emotional resilience. When you engage in healthy self-soothing techniques, you activate your brain's dopamine pathways, creating a sense of well-being and reinforcing the habit of emotional regulation.

For those who grew up in environments where emotional support was inconsistent or absent, self-soothing can feel foreign or unnatural. Attachment theory suggests that children who did not experience consistent nurturing often struggle with self-regulation as adults. However, regardless of your past experiences, you can learn these skills and begin to create a sense of emotional safety within yourself.

Take John, for example. After a long and stressful day at work, his first instinct was to drown his frustration in alcohol or hours of mindless TV. But as he began learning about self-soothing, he decided to try a different approach. Instead of escaping his feelings, he drew a warm bath with lavender oil, allowing the calming scent and warmth to soothe his body and mind. As he lay in the water, he practiced slow, deep breathing, grounding himself in the present. Over time, this became a habit—one that allowed him to unwind without self-destruction.

If you've struggled with self-soothing in the past, know that it's never too late to build new habits. Your brain is capable of adapting and learning new ways to handle emotions, no matter how deeply ingrained old patterns may be.

Therapeutic Strategies for Self-Soothing

The key to self-soothing is finding practices that resonate with you—activities that bring comfort, regulate emotions, and create a sense of safety within. Experimenting with different techniques will help you discover what works best for your unique emotional needs.

Breathing as a Path to Calm: The Power of Mindful Breathwork

Sometimes, the simplest solutions are the most powerful. In moments of emotional turbulence—when thoughts spiral and your body tenses—the act of conscious breathing can serve as an anchor, bringing you back to the present moment.

Breathing is more than just a biological function—it is a direct line to your nervous system. The way you breathe can either reinforce stress or invite relaxation. When emotions run high, your body instinctively shifts into fight-or-flight mode, quickening your breath, increasing your heart rate, and preparing for perceived danger. While this response is useful in emergencies, it often hijacks your emotional well-being in everyday situations, like conflict with a loved one or workplace stress.

Mindful breathing helps override this automatic reaction, sending signals to your brain that you are safe. By engaging in intentional breathwork, you can regulate your nervous system, slow down anxious thoughts, and cultivate a sense of calm—even in the middle of chaos.

If you find yourself caught in emotional overwhelm, try these simple breathing techniques:

- 4-7-8 Breathing: Inhale for 4 seconds, hold for 7 seconds, and exhale slowly for 8 seconds. This helps reduce stress and activate your body's relaxation response.

- Box Breathing: Inhale for 4 seconds, hold for 4 seconds, exhale for 4 seconds, and hold again for 4 seconds. This technique helps restore balance and focus.
- Diaphragmatic Breathing: Place one hand on your belly and the other on your chest. As you inhale, allow your belly to expand fully. As you exhale, feel your belly contract. This deep breathing method engages your parasympathetic nervous system, promoting relaxation.

Practicing just a few minutes of mindful breathing each day can rewire your brain's stress response, making it easier to self-soothe and regain emotional clarity.

Embracing Self-Soothing as a Lifelong Practice

Learning to self-soothe is not about eliminating negative emotions—it's about learning how to ride the waves of emotion without being overwhelmed by them. Every time you practice a self-soothing technique, you are strengthening new neural pathways, making it easier to regulate emotions and find peace within yourself.

As you explore different self-soothing strategies, ask yourself:

- What calms me when I feel overwhelmed?
- How can I create moments of peace and grounding in my daily life?
- What small step can I take today to prioritize emotional regulation?

Healing happens one step at a time. Each time you pause instead of reacting impulsively, choose a grounding technique, or remind yourself that you are safe, you are reinforcing a new way of relating to your emotions. Over time, these small changes add up, paving the way for greater emotional balance and resilience.

No matter where you are in your journey, know this: you are capable of finding calm within.

The 4-7-8 Breathing Method: Engaging the Body's Natural Relaxation Response

One of the most effective breathing techniques for reducing anxiety and promoting deep relaxation is the **4-7-8 method**. Developed by Dr. Andrew Weil, this technique encourages slow, rhythmic breathing, naturally slowing the heart rate and reducing tension. If you have trouble remembering the numbers, don't panic. Just take a deep breath, hold it for a while and then slowly exhale. Repeat.

To practice 4-7-8 breathing:

- Inhale deeply through your nose for a count of four. Feel your belly expand as you take in air.
- Hold your breath for a count of seven. This brief pause allows oxygen to circulate through your bloodstream.
- Exhale slowly through your mouth for a count of eight. Focus on releasing any tension with the breath.

Repeating this cycle three to four times can create an immediate sense of calm, making it an excellent tool for managing stress, easing anxiety, or preparing for sleep.

For Emily, who struggled with nighttime anxiety, this practice became a lifeline. Instead of lying awake with racing thoughts, she turned to 4-7-8 breathing, allowing the steady rhythm to lull her body into a restful state. Over time, she found that this simple technique not only improved her sleep but also made her more resilient to stress throughout the day.

Box Breathing: A Structured Approach to Mindful Breathing

If you often find yourself caught in rapid, shallow breathing—especially during stressful situations—**box breathing** can help restore balance. This method, used by Navy SEALs to maintain composure under pressure, involves **four equal phases of breath**, creating a structured rhythm that calms the mind and body.

To practice box breathing:

- Inhale deeply through your nose for four counts.
- Hold the breath for four counts, allowing stillness to settle.
- Exhale fully through your mouth for four counts, releasing tension.
- Hold the exhale for four counts before beginning again.

Visualizing a box—tracing each side with your breath—can make this practice even more effective. As you breathe in, imagine moving up one side of the box. As you hold, trace across. Exhaling takes you down the other side, and the final hold completes the shape.

For Mark, who often felt overwhelmed in social situations, box breathing became his go-to grounding technique. Before entering meetings or engaging in difficult conversations, he would discreetly practice a few cycles, allowing his nervous system to settle. What once felt like paralyzing anxiety became manageable, simply by using his breath as a tool.

Biblical Insight: The Breath of Life

"The Spirit of God has made me; the breath of the Almighty gives me life." (Job 33:4)

Breath has always been sacred. In scripture, it is the very breath of God that gives life, symbolizing renewal, presence, and peace. When you engage in mindful breathing, you are not just calming your body—you are reconnecting with the source of life itself.

Takeaway Action: Breathe with Intention

Mindful breathing is a practice that can be integrated into daily life. Whether you're preparing for a stressful event, winding down after a long day, or simply seeking a moment of stillness, your breath is always available as a tool for **grounding, calming, and restoring balance**.

- Set aside three minutes each day to practice 4-7-8 or box breathing.
- Use breathwork as a reset before reacting to stress or conflict.
- Experiment with different breathing techniques to discover what works best for you.

By training yourself to breathe with awareness, you cultivate a sense of **inner stability**, allowing you to face challenges with clarity and composure. So, take a deep breath—**your healing begins...**

Creativity as a Path to Emotional Healing

Emotions can sometimes feel too complex to articulate, too overwhelming to explain. In these moments, creativity becomes a powerful outlet—an unspoken language that allows us to process what words cannot. Whether through painting, writing, or music, creative expression provides a pathway to release, understand, and transform difficult emotions.

Think of a time when you felt emotionally stuck—perhaps burdened by stress, sadness, or frustration. Did you instinctively turn to a song that resonated with your mood? Did you ever find solace in scribbling thoughts into a notebook or absentmindedly doodling on paper? These simple acts are not meaningless; they are forms of self-soothing, helping to externalize emotions and bring a sense of relief.

For those struggling with emotional dysregulation, creative expression offers a safe and structured way to process intense feelings. It shifts the focus from internal chaos to outward creation, allowing emotions to flow rather than become bottled up.

Journaling: Writing Your Way to Clarity

When emotions feel tangled and overwhelming, journaling can serve as a lifeline. The act of putting thoughts onto paper helps slow racing thoughts, providing clarity and emotional release.

Consider Emily, who often found herself spiraling into anxiety after difficult conversations. When she started journaling, she gave herself permission to pour out her unfiltered emotions without fear of judgment. Over time, she noticed patterns in her triggers and responses. Instead of reacting impulsively, she learned to pause, reflect, and approach situations with greater awareness.

If you're new to journaling, start small:

Set a timer for five minutes and write whatever comes to mind. Don't worry about grammar or structure—just let your thoughts flow.

If you feel stuck, use prompts such as:

- What emotion am I feeling most strongly right now?
- What triggered this feeling, and how can I respond differently next time?
- What do I need to hear in this moment to feel supported?

With consistency, journaling can become a trusted tool for emotional processing, helping you untangle your thoughts and regain a sense of control.

Art Therapy: Healing Through Visual Expression

Not all emotions can be neatly packaged into words. Sometimes, they manifest as colors, shapes, and movement—expressions that feel more natural than verbal explanations.

Engaging in art therapy allows you to express your inner world without the pressure of finding the "right" words. The process itself, rather than the final product, is what heals.

Take David, who struggled with unresolved grief. Talking about his pain felt impossible, but when he picked up a paintbrush, he found a way to express it. The act of painting became a meditative practice, helping him externalize his sorrow and process it in a way that felt safe.

If you'd like to explore art therapy, try:

- Doodling or sketching whatever comes to mind, without judgment.
- Painting your emotions using colors that reflect your mood.
- Coloring mandalas as a form of meditation, allowing the repetitive patterns to quiet your mind.

Even if you don't consider yourself an artist, engaging with visual expression can be deeply therapeutic, offering a nonverbal outlet for emotional release.

Music: Letting Sound Guide Your Emotions

Music has a profound ability to mirror and shift our emotions. Certain songs evoke memories, soothe anxieties, or provide an outlet for unexpressed feelings.

If you're feeling emotionally overwhelmed, try using music as a tool for regulation:

Match your mood first. If you're feeling sad, start with a song that reflects that sadness. This validates your emotions rather than suppressing them.

Gradually shift to soothing melodies. Slowly transition to music that promotes calmness, allowing your nervous system to regulate.

Sing or play an instrument. If you enjoy singing or playing music, use it as a direct emotional outlet. Even humming can activate the vagus nerve, which promotes relaxation.

For Rachel, who often felt anxious after work, playing the piano became her sanctuary. The rhythmic movement of her hands across the keys gave her a sense of control, transforming her stress into something tangible. Over time, she noticed a significant decrease in her anxiety, as playing music provided both structure and emotional release.

Biblical Insight: The Healing Power of Creativity

"He has put a new song in my mouth—praise to our God." (Psalm 40:3)

Throughout the Bible, creative expression—whether through song, poetry, or craftsmanship—has been a means of both worship and healing. David wrote psalms to process his struggles. The Israelites used music to express joy and lament. Creativity has always been a divine gift, offering a way to navigate the highs and lows of life. In moments of distress, embrace the creative outlets available to you. Whether through journaling, painting, or music, allow yourself to engage with the healing power of artistic expression.

Reconnecting with Nature: A Path to Inner Peace

In the modern world, it's easy to feel disconnected—from ourselves, from others, and from the natural rhythms of life. We spend hours staring at screens, navigating crowded spaces, and juggling responsibilities that leave us feeling drained. Yet, there is a simple, ancient remedy that has the power to restore balance: nature. Spending time outdoors isn't just about enjoying a scenic view—it is a scientifically proven way to reduce stress, lower cortisol levels, and promote emotional well-being. Nature has a grounding effect, reminding us to slow down, breathe deeply, and reconnect with something larger than ourselves.

The Science of Nature's Healing Power

Research in psychology and neuroscience consistently confirms what many of us instinctively feel—being in nature calms the nervous system and enhances overall mental health. When we immerse ourselves in a natural setting, our bodies respond in profound ways:

- Lowered Cortisol Levels: Studies show that spending just 20 minutes in nature can significantly reduce cortisol, the stress hormone responsible for anxiety and tension.
- Improved Mood: Exposure to natural environments increases the production of serotonin and dopamine, neurotransmitters that boost happiness and relaxation.
- Enhanced Cognitive Function: Time outdoors can improve focus, memory, and creativity, making it an essential tool for mental clarity.

Consider Lisa, who often felt overwhelmed by the constant noise of city life. Between work deadlines, social obligations, and endless notifications on her phone, she rarely had a moment to breathe. One day, feeling particularly drained, she decided to visit a nearby park. She left her phone in her bag and focused on the feeling of her feet touching the earth, the rustling of leaves, and the warmth of the sun on her skin. To her surprise, just thirty minutes of being present in nature left her feeling lighter, more focused, and at peace. Nature didn't change her responsibilities, but it changed how she carried them.

Simple Ways to Connect with Nature

You don't have to go on a grand hiking expedition to experience the benefits of the natural world. Even small, intentional moments spent in nature can ground your emotions, improve your well-being, and bring clarity to your mind.

1. Take a Mindful Walk

Walking is one of the most accessible ways to reset your nervous system. The key is to be fully present rather than rushing through the experience.

As you walk, engage your senses:

- Notice the rhythm of your steps, the gentle impact of your feet on the ground.
- Listen to the rustling of the leaves, birdsong, or the distant hum of the wind.
- Feel the temperature of the air, the sunlight on your skin, or the coolness of the breeze.

By focusing on these sensations, you shift your attention away from stress and into the present moment, allowing nature to recalibrate your mind and body.

For Mark, an overworked executive, taking daily walks became a lifeline. At first, he thought it was a waste of time—his inbox was always full, his responsibilities endless. But as he committed to 20 minutes of outdoor movement each day, he noticed something shift. His anxiety lessened, his thinking became clearer, and he felt more in control of his emotions. Nature became his reset button, allowing him to return to work with a renewed sense of purpose and calm.

2. Bring Nature Indoors

If getting outside isn't always an option, you can still experience the calming effects of nature by bringing elements of it into your home or workspace.

- Surround yourself with plants: Studies show that indoor plants improve air quality and reduce stress. Even a small potted plant on your desk can make a difference.
- Listen to nature sounds: The sound of rain, ocean waves, or a forest breeze can have a deeply soothing effect, helping you feel more at peace even in the middle of a busy day.
- Use natural light: Whenever possible, open your curtains and let sunlight fill your space. Exposure to natural light improves mood and regulates your body's internal clock.

Sarah, who lived in a high-rise apartment and worked long hours, found that keeping plants around her home helped her feel more connected to nature. She also started playing nature sounds while she worked, finding that the soft hum of a waterfall or birdsong eased her tension and improved her focus. Even though she couldn't always be outdoors, these small changes made her environment feel more peaceful and restorative.

Biblical Insight: Finding God in Nature

"The heavens declare the glory of God; the skies proclaim the work of His hands." (Psalm 19:1)

Nature is a reflection of divine creation, a reminder that we are part of something vast and beautiful. Throughout scripture, we see moments where God meets people in nature—Moses on the mountain, Elijah in the wilderness, Jesus praying in solitude. These moments remind us that stillness and connection with nature are essential for spiritual renewal. When you step into nature, whether it's a grand landscape or a quiet corner of a park, take a moment to reflect. What does God's creation reveal to you about peace, presence, and renewal?

Reconnect with the Natural World

Nature has the power to restore, refresh, and rebalance your emotions. Whether you have five minutes or an entire afternoon, prioritize moments that bring you closer to the natural world.

- Go outside daily, even if just for a short walk.
- Pay attention to your senses—sight, sound, smell, touch—to fully experience nature.

- Bring nature indoors through plants, natural light, or soothing nature sounds.

The next time you feel overwhelmed, step outside, breathe deeply, and allow the natural world to remind you: you are grounded, you are connected, and you are whole.

Cultivating Self-Compassion: Learning to Be Kind to Yourself

For many people struggling with emotional dysregulation, self-criticism becomes an ingrained habit. Instead of responding to mistakes or setbacks with patience and understanding, they may resort to harsh inner dialogue, believing that self-punishment is the path to self-improvement. However, research in psychology tells us the opposite—self-compassion, not self-judgment, is the key to resilience and growth.

Self-compassion is the practice of treating yourself with the same kindness, patience, and encouragement that you would offer to a close friend. It is not self-pity, nor is it an excuse to avoid responsibility. Instead, it is a way of acknowledging your struggles with gentleness and grace, allowing you to move forward with clarity and strength. If you tend to be your own worst critic, it may be time to reframe your relationship with yourself—not through perfectionism or punishment, but through understanding and self-kindness.

The Science of Self-Compassion

Psychologist Dr. Kristin Neff[9], a leading researcher on self-compassion, has found that practicing self-kindness leads to lower anxiety, increased motivation, and greater emotional resilience. She outlines three essential components of self-compassion:

- Self-Kindness vs. Self-Judgment – Instead of beating yourself up for mistakes, offer yourself the same encouragement and patience you would give a friend.
- Common Humanity vs. Isolation – Recognize that imperfection is part of the human experience. You are not alone in your struggles.
- Mindfulness vs. Over-Identification – Acknowledge your emotions without letting them define you. Learn to observe your pain without getting lost in it.

Consider Emily, who made a mistake at work and immediately spiraled into self-criticism. Her inner voice was cruel: *"I always mess up. I'm such a failure. Everyone must think I'm incompetent."* These thoughts didn't help her improve; they only increased her anxiety and self-doubt.

Now, imagine if Emily had responded with self-compassion instead: *"I made a mistake, but that doesn't define me. Everyone makes errors sometimes. I'll learn from this and move forward."* This shift in thinking allows her to learn without shame and move forward without carrying unnecessary emotional weight. The way we speak to ourselves matters. When we replace self-judgment with self-kindness, we build emotional resilience and foster inner healing.

Practical Self-Compassion Exercises

If you struggle with self-criticism, try these evidence-based self-compassion techniques to develop a more supportive and nurturing inner voice.

1. The "Talk to Yourself Like a Friend" Technique

The next time you catch yourself thinking, *I'm such a failure* or *I can't do anything right*, pause. Ask yourself:

"Would I say this to a close friend if they were struggling?"

Chances are, you wouldn't. Instead of shaming them, you'd offer reassurance, perspective, and kindness. Now, apply that same kindness to yourself.

- Instead of: "I'll never get this right."
- Try: "I'm still learning, and mistakes are part of growth."
- Instead of: "I'm so unlovable."
- Try: "Everyone struggles with self-doubt sometimes, but I am worthy of love and connection."

Practicing gentle, supportive self-talk will rewire your brain over time, making self-compassion your default response rather than self-criticism.

2. Progressive Muscle Relaxation (PMR) for Emotional Grounding

When stress builds up in your body, it often manifests as tension in your muscles, making it harder to regulate emotions. Progressive Muscle Relaxation (PMR) is a powerful self-soothing technique that helps release physical tension while promoting a sense of calm and presence.

How to Practice PMR:

- Find a quiet space where you can sit or lie down comfortably.

- Start with your toes: Inhale deeply, tense the muscles in your feet for five seconds, then exhale as you release.
- Move up to your calves, then your thighs, stomach, shoulders, and jaw, repeating the process.
- As you relax each muscle group, focus on the sensation of release, allowing your body to let go of stored tension.

Imagine Julia, who often feels overwhelmed by anxiety. When she starts practicing PMR at night, she notices an immediate difference—her racing thoughts slow down, her breathing deepens, and her body feels lighter. This simple practice becomes her anchor, a ritual that signals her nervous system to shift into a state of calm.

If you struggle with chronic stress, try incorporating PMR into your daily routine. It can be particularly effective before bedtime or during moments of emotional distress.

3. **Self-Compassionate Journaling**

Journaling is a powerful tool for self-reflection and emotional healing. It allows you to process your emotions without judgment and reframe negative thoughts with a more balanced perspective.

Try this simple journaling exercise:

- Describe a recent challenge you faced and how it made you feel.
- Identify the self-judgment that arose—what negative thoughts did you have about yourself?

- Reframe the narrative by writing a compassionate response to yourself. Imagine you are comforting a friend in the same situation.

For example, if you write:

> "I felt rejected when my friend canceled our plans. I immediately thought, 'They don't care about me.'"

You might reframe it with:

> "Maybe they had a tough day and needed rest. Their cancellation doesn't mean I'm unimportant. I am worthy of connection, and one canceled plan doesn't define my friendships."

By practicing self-compassionate journaling, you train your brain to see challenges through a kinder, more forgiving lens.

Biblical Insight: Embracing Grace and Compassion

> "The Lord is compassionate and gracious, slow to anger, abounding in love." (Psalm 103:8)

Self-compassion aligns with the divine invitation to embrace grace rather than condemnation. If God extends unconditional love and mercy, why should we withhold it from ourselves? When you find yourself caught in a cycle of self-criticism, remind yourself that you are worthy of kindness, patience, and love—just as you are.

Takeaway Action: Start Practicing Self-Compassion Today

Breaking the habit of self-judgment takes time, patience, and practice. Choose one of the self-compassion techniques outlined above and commit to integrating it into your daily life.

- Pause and reframe negative thoughts—speak to yourself as you would a friend.
- Practice PMR whenever you feel overwhelmed.
- Start a self-compassion journal to track your progress and shift your inner dialogue.

The next time you make a mistake, instead of criticizing yourself, pause. Take a deep breath and say:

> "I am human. I am learning. And I am worthy of kindness—especially from myself."

Creating Soothing Rituals: Building Stability Through Routine

Your nervous system thrives on predictability and consistency. When you incorporate soothing rituals into your daily routine, you send a powerful message to your body and mind: You are safe. You are cared for. You can rest. If you struggle with emotional dysregulation, developing structured self-soothing habits can provide a much-needed sense of stability, helping you regulate emotions more effectively.

Think about a time when you felt overwhelmed or emotionally drained. How did you respond? Did you instinctively reach for distractions—scrolling endlessly through social media, turning to comfort foods, or zoning out in front of the TV? While these behaviors may temporarily numb discomfort, they do not provide true emotional regulation. They simply delay and suppress emotions, often leaving you feeling just as unsettled—if not worse—once the distraction fades.

Now, imagine a different approach. Instead of reacting to stress after it arises, what if you proactively wove calming rituals into your daily life? Simple yet intentional routines that signal safety to your nervous system and build a foundation of inner peace. These rituals don't need to be elaborate—just small, consistent moments of self-care that help ground you before stress even takes hold.

By committing to soothing rituals, you give yourself the gift of emotional steadiness and resilience, creating a life where peace is not just something you seek after chaos—but something you cultivate every day.

The Science of Soothing Rituals: How Predictability Regulates the Nervous System

Research in neuroscience and behavioral psychology confirms that predictable routines help regulate the nervous system. When you engage in habitual soothing practices, your brain begins to associate these rituals with safety and relaxation, making it easier to return to a state of emotional balance during stressful moments.

Dr. Bruce Perry[10], a leading trauma expert, explains that rhythmic and repetitive activities—such as structured routines, deep breathing, and movement—help rewire the brain, shifting it out of survival mode and into a state of regulation. When you establish consistent, calming habits, you reduce emotional volatility and build a stronger foundation for resilience and self-regulation.

Practical Strategies for Establishing Soothing Rituals

If you struggle with emotional overwhelm, incorporating simple but intentional rituals into your daily routine can help train your nervous system to associate specific actions with relaxation. Over time, these practices rewire your brain, making it easier to manage stress, regulate emotions, and restore balance.

1. Creating a Bedtime Routine for Emotional Restoration

A well-structured bedtime routine is one of the most powerful ways to train your nervous system to regulate stress and improve emotional resilience. Sleep is not just physical rest—it is psychological repair. The quality of your sleep impacts your mood, stress tolerance, and cognitive clarity.

If you struggle with emotional dysregulation, bedtime might feel like a battle—racing thoughts, restlessness, or emotional processing that keeps you awake. Establishing a calming nighttime ritual can help signal to your brain that it is time to unwind.

Try incorporating the following into your evening routine:

- **Limit screen time before bed** to reduce cortisol spikes and encourage melatonin production.
- **Engage in a calming practice** such as reading, gentle stretching, or deep breathing exercises.
- **Create a sensory cue for relaxation**—dim the lights, use lavender essential oil, or listen to soft music.
- **Maintain a consistent sleep schedule**, reinforcing predictability for your nervous system.

By establishing a structured bedtime ritual, you create a sense of stability, making it easier to regulate emotions and face each day with greater clarity and resilience.

Imagine Sophia, who used to struggle with racing thoughts at night. She found that lighting a candle, drinking chamomile tea, and reading a book in bed helped her shift from anxious overthinking to restful relaxation. Over time, these habits transformed her nights from restless tossing and turning to deep, restorative sleep.

2. Scheduling Daily Mini-Retreats for the Nervous System

Just as your body needs food throughout the day, your nervous system needs moments of emotional rest. Setting aside just 10 minutes a day for intentional relaxation can reset your stress levels and help prevent emotional burnout.

Consider integrating these mini-retreats into your day:

- Morning grounding: Start the day with prayer, meditation, or deep breathing to center yourself before engaging with the world.
- Afternoon reset: Step outside for a short walk or engage in gentle stretching to release tension.
- Evening wind-down: Engage in self-massage, progressive muscle relaxation, or calming music to transition into a state of rest.

Think of these rituals as emotional "pit stops"—opportunities to recharge and reset rather than push through stress without relief.

3. Engaging in Mindful Movement

Movement is one of the most effective ways to regulate the nervous system and release built-up emotional energy. The key is to choose activities that feel gentle, grounding, and rhythmic.

Try incorporating mindful movement into your routine:

- Stretching or yoga to release muscle tension and promote relaxation.
- Taking a walk outside while focusing on the sensation of your feet on the ground.
- Swaying or rocking movements, which mimic the soothing effects of being cradled.

Research shows that repetitive, rhythmic movements (such as walking, stretching, or slow dancing) activate the brain's parasympathetic nervous system, shifting the body from stress to calm.

Consider James, who struggled with emotional outbursts at work. Instead of bottling up his frustration, he started taking 10-minute walks during his breaks. The simple act of walking, breathing deeply, and feeling the fresh air helped him reset his emotions, making him less reactive throughout the day.

4. Finding Comfort in Spiritual Rest

Beyond physical relaxation, true rest comes from inner peace and spiritual grounding. In moments of distress, many find deep comfort in prayer, scripture, or meditative reflection.

Biblical wisdom reminds us of the importance of seeking peace beyond mere distraction:

"Come to me, all you who are weary and burdened, and I will give you rest." (Matthew 11:28)

This passage reminds us that self-soothing is not just about temporary relaxation—it's about seeking lasting peace. Turning to prayer, meditation, or scripture can help you feel emotionally anchored, reinforcing that peace is found not in avoidance, but in surrender.

Consider adding these spiritual self-soothing practices to your day:

- Morning devotional time—reading scripture or journaling your thoughts and prayers.
- Silent meditation or contemplative prayer—sitting quietly, allowing your mind to settle.

- Reciting affirmations rooted in faith—such as, "I am held in God's peace" or "I trust that I am loved and supported."

Imagine Rebecca, who often felt overwhelmed by anxiety. She began setting aside 15 minutes in the morning to read Psalms, pray, and journal. This small shift transformed her day, allowing her to approach challenges with greater clarity, peace, and resilience.

Takeaway: Start Small and Build Consistency

Developing soothing rituals is not about overhauling your entire routine overnight—it's about small, intentional shifts that create lasting emotional stability.

Start by choosing just ONE soothing ritual to integrate into your daily life.

- If you struggle with anxiety at night, establish a bedtime wind-down routine with herbal tea and journaling.
- If you feel emotionally drained mid-day, take a 10-minute break for mindful breathing or stretching.
- If you crave deeper peace, incorporate spiritual self-care, such as prayer or scripture reading.

Each small step reinforces your nervous system that you are safe, supported, and capable of emotional regulation. Over time, these rituals become second nature—your personal sanctuary amidst the chaos of life. The journey toward emotional healing and balance begins with one simple act of self-care.

Cognitive Restructuring: Rewiring the Mind for Emotional Clarity

While self-soothing techniques help regulate emotions in the moment, true healing requires addressing the thought patterns that fuel emotional dysregulation. Many of your strongest emotional reactions don't stem from events themselves but from the way you interpret them. When you repeatedly engage in distorted or unhelpful thinking, you reinforce negative emotional cycles, making it harder to respond with clarity and calm.

This process of changing unhelpful thought patterns is known as cognitive restructuring—a technique that helps you identify, challenge, and replace irrational beliefs with more balanced, constructive perspectives. Learning to reshape these automatic thoughts is essential for reducing anxiety, managing anger, and fostering emotional stability.

Understanding Cognitive Distortions: How Thoughts Shape Reality

Your mind is incredibly powerful, but it is also prone to cognitive distortions—habitual thinking patterns that reinforce anxiety, depression, and emotional instability. These distortions often develop from past experiences, trauma, or deeply ingrained beliefs, shaping the way you perceive reality.

Recognizing these distortions is the first step toward breaking free from reactive thinking and developing emotional clarity.

1. Black-and-White Thinking: When Nuance Disappears

Black-and-white thinking causes you to see situations in extremes, leaving no room for middle ground. Everything is either a success or a failure, good or bad, with no consideration for nuance or progress.

Consider Laura. After making a small mistake at work, she tells herself, *"I'm terrible at my job. I'll never succeed."* One misstep erases all of her achievements, leaving her feeling defeated and incapable.

- Cognitive Shift: Instead of thinking, I'm a failure, Laura practices reframing:

    "I made a mistake, but I've also done many things well. One mistake does not define me."

By challenging all-or-nothing thinking, Laura allows room for growth and self-compassion.

2. Catastrophizing: Imagining the Worst-Case Scenario

Catastrophizing happens when you assume the worst possible outcome, amplifying fear and anxiety.

Take James, for example. After a job interview, he thinks, *"I stumbled on one answer. I'll never get the job. I'll be unemployed forever."* His fear-driven thoughts spiral, making it impossible to see a realistic perspective.

- Cognitive Shift: Instead of spiraling into worst-case scenarios, James asks himself:

> *"Is this fact or fear? One mistake doesn't mean I won't get the job. Even if I don't, I have other opportunities."*

By grounding his thoughts in reality, James prevents anxiety from distorting his perception.

3. Personalization: Taking on Blame That Isn't Yours

Personalization leads you to assume responsibility for things beyond your control, often causing guilt and over-apologizing.

Maria notices that her friend is acting distant and immediately assumes, "*I must have done something wrong.*" Instead of considering that her friend might be dealing with unrelated stress, Maria internalizes blame, making herself responsible for emotions that aren't hers to carry.

- Cognitive Shift: Instead of assuming blame, Maria reminds herself:

    > *"My friend might be going through something unrelated to me. I can check in, but I don't need to take responsibility for her emotions."*

By **challenging personalization**, Maria is able to **support her friend without carrying unnecessary emotional weight**.

The Power of Cognitive Restructuring

When you learn to challenge cognitive distortions, you take back control over how you experience emotions and navigate relationships. The goal isn't to ignore feelings but to see them through a clearer, more balanced lens.

Each time you pause, challenge an irrational thought, and replace it with a more constructive perspective, you rewire your brain for emotional stability and resilience.

Start by reflecting:

- Where in your life do you see patterns of black-and-white thinking, catastrophizing, or personalization?
- What small shifts can you make today to reshape the way you interpret challenges?
- How can you remind yourself that thoughts are not facts—they can be examined, adjusted, and redefined?

By practicing cognitive restructuring, you create space for growth, confidence, and a more balanced emotional life.

Rewiring Thought Patterns: A Practical Approach

Meet Sarah. Anytime her boss gave her constructive feedback, she panicked, convinced she was about to be fired. Her fear wasn't based on reality—it stemmed from an old belief that criticism meant rejection. Through **cognitive restructuring**, Sarah learned to **challenge her initial reaction**. Instead of assuming, *"I'm incompetent"*, she asked herself, *"Is there actual evidence for this thought?"*

Through reflection, she realized:

- Her boss had never suggested she was in danger of losing her job.
- Feedback was normal and even helpful.
- Her fear was a learned response from past experiences, not an accurate reflection of her current situation.

By rewiring her thought process, Sarah reduced her emotional reactivity and learned to view feedback as an opportunity for growth rather than a personal attack.

Therapeutic Strategies for Cognitive Restructuring

If you struggle with negative thought patterns, these practical exercises can help you shift your mindset and develop emotional resilience.

1. Thought Journaling: Identifying & Reframing Negative Thoughts

Each time you experience a strong emotional reaction, take a few moments to write down:

- What triggered it? (What was the event or situation?)
- What thoughts went through your mind? (How did you interpret it?)
- Is this thought accurate, or am I making assumptions?
- What is a more balanced way to view this situation?

Example:

Trigger: My friend didn't text me back.

Thought: She must be mad at me.

Balanced Perspective: Maybe she's just busy. I can check in instead of assuming.

Over time, journaling helps reveal patterns in your thinking, making it easier to challenge and reframe automatic negative thoughts.

2. The Socratic Method: Challenging Irrational Thoughts

The **Socratic Method** is a powerful tool for **breaking down cognitive distortions**. When a negative thought arises, ask yourself:

- What's the evidence for and against this thought?
- Am I making assumptions or jumping to conclusions?
- How would I view this situation if I were feeling calm?
- What would I tell a friend if they had this thought?

By challenging irrational thoughts, you create mental space for a more objective and healthier perspective.

3. Positive Reframing: Changing Self-Talk

The way you speak to yourself has a profound impact on your emotions. Replacing negative self-talk with constructive language can retrain your brain to respond with resilience instead of fear.

- Instead of saying:

    I can't handle this.

    I always mess up.

    Nobody cares about me.

- Try reframing it to:

    This is difficult, but I've overcome challenges before.

    I made a mistake, but I can learn from it.

I am loved and supported, even if I can't see it right now.

Each time you consciously reframe a negative thought, you strengthen new neural pathways, making balanced thinking a natural habit over time.

Biblical Insight: Taking Control of Your Thoughts

"Take captive every thought to make it obedient to Christ." (2 Corinthians 10:5)

This verse reminds us that our minds shape our reality. By intentionally directing our thoughts toward truth and hope, we align ourselves with a mindset that fosters emotional clarity and resilience.

Applying These Lessons: Taking the First Step

Healing is not a passive experience—it is an intentional process that requires both immediate emotional relief and long-term mindset shifts. It begins with small, consistent steps that retrain your mind, rewire your emotions, and restore balance to your daily life.

As you move forward, consider how you can integrate these principles into your everyday routine. Healing is not about perfection but about progress, and each intentional step brings you closer to inner peace, emotional clarity, and stronger relationships.

Choose One Self-Soothing Strategy for Emotional Regulation

When emotions feel overwhelming, having a self-soothing tool at your disposal can help you regain control in the moment. Instead of reacting impulsively to distress, practice engaging in an activity that soothes your nervous system and creates a sense of internal safety.

Your thoughts shape how you see the world, how you feel about yourself, and how you respond to challenges. Yet, for many, negative thoughts feel automatic—a constant whisper of doubt and self-criticism running in the background of everyday life. If left unchecked, these thoughts can distort reality, making it difficult to see situations clearly or respond with resilience. But here's the truth: You are not at the mercy of these thoughts. By learning to pause, examine, and reframe them, you can reshape your inner narrative, shifting from self-doubt to self-compassion, from fear to confidence, and from negativity to empowerment.

Reframing your inner dialogue is not about ignoring challenges or pretending everything is positive—it's about challenging distorted thinking and replacing it with a more balanced, constructive perspective. When you learn to question unhelpful thoughts and replace them with truth, you give yourself the ability to respond to life with clarity, confidence, and emotional strength. This process takes practice, but each time you choose to challenge a limiting belief, you reinforce a healthier, more resilient mindset. With time, the voice of doubt fades, and a new voice—one rooted in strength, wisdom, and self-worth—takes its place.

One of the most effective ways to do this is through the ***Socratic Method***, a process of questioning that helps you deconstruct irrational beliefs and replace them with truth-based, balanced perspectives.

Imagine you're facing a situation where self-doubt creeps in. Perhaps you made a mistake at work, and suddenly, your mind jumps to a familiar negative script: *I always mess up. I'm going to lose my job.* Before you spiral into anxiety, pause. Instead of accepting the thought as truth, begin questioning it like a detective searching for real evidence:

- What evidence supports this thought? Is there actual proof that one mistake means I'm incompetent, or is this an assumption?
- Am I assuming the worst without proof? Has anyone suggested I'm losing my job, or am I catastrophizing?
- What's a more balanced way to interpret this situation? Instead of I always mess up, could I reframe it as, I made a mistake, but I've also done a lot of things well. I can learn from this and move forward?

This simple act of challenging and reframing thoughts creates space for logic to take over where fear and self-doubt once ruled.

Rewriting the Story: Thought Journaling for Clarity

For many, negative thoughts are so ingrained that they operate beneath conscious awareness. They show up in moments of stress, disappointment, or uncertainty, influencing emotions before we even recognize what's happening. To disrupt this cycle, writing them down can be a powerful tool.

Thought journaling helps you bring awareness to negative patterns, recognize distortions, and practice reframing in real time. The next time you experience a strong emotional reaction to a thought, try this exercise:

- Write down the distressing thought as it first appeared in your mind. Be as specific as possible.
- Identify the distortion at play. Are you catastrophizing, personalizing, or engaging in black-and-white thinking?
- Challenge the thought using the Socratic Method. What actual evidence do you have to support or contradict it?
- Reframe it into a more constructive, truth-based perspective. How would you interpret this situation if you were feeling calm and self-compassionate?

Consider this example:

- Original Thought: My friend didn't text me back—she must be mad at me.
- Cognitive Distortion: Personalization and mind-reading (assuming you know what someone else is thinking).
- Reframed Thought: There are many reasons she might not have responded yet. She could be busy or distracted. I'll give it time instead of jumping to conclusions.

By consistently journaling thoughts in this way, you train your brain to automatically engage in healthier, more balanced thinking rather than falling into familiar negative loops.

Replacing Negative Self-Talk with Daily Affirmations

What you say to yourself matters. If you constantly engage in self-criticism, you reinforce neural pathways that make negative thinking a habit. But if you intentionally replace those thoughts with affirmations, you can rewire your brain for self-compassion and resilience.

Think about how you speak to yourself in difficult moments. When you fail, do you immediately think, *I'm such a failure?* When you face rejection, do you conclude, *I'm not good enough?* Now, imagine if you spoke to yourself with the same kindness you would offer a close friend.

Affirmations are short, positive statements that challenge negative self-talk and reinforce truth.

- Try incorporating them into your daily routine:
- Each morning, say an affirmation aloud in front of the mirror.
- Write them down in a journal before bed, reinforcing positive self-perceptions.
- When a negative thought arises, counter it with a specific affirmation that aligns with the truth.
- Here are some affirmations to help replace negative self-talk:
  - *I am capable of growth and change.*
  - *A single mistake does not define my worth.*
  - *I choose to see my challenges as opportunities for learning.*
  - *I am deserving of love, success, and happiness.*
  - *Every day, I am becoming stronger and wiser.*

If negative thoughts feel overwhelming, choose one affirmation that resonates with you and repeat it throughout the day. Over time, these affirmations will reshape your internal dialogue, helping you build confidence and emotional resilience.

Shifting Your Mindset: The Power of Reframing

Every challenge, setback, and moment of self-doubt presents a choice: You can let it define you, or you can reframe it as an opportunity for growth.

> Instead of saying, *I can't handle this,* try, *This is difficult, but I have faced challenges before and survived.*

> Instead of thinking, *This failure proves I'm not good enough,* remind yourself, *Failure is part of success. What can I learn from this?*

By practicing reframing, you take control of the story you tell yourself—and when you change the story, you change the outcome.

Putting It Into Practice

Your thoughts create emotions. Your emotions shape behaviors. And your behaviors determine the quality of your life. If you want to change how you feel and act, start by changing how you think.

Take a moment to reflect:

- What is one recurring negative thought you struggle with?
- How can you begin questioning its validity?
- Which affirmation will you commit to repeating daily?

Healing and growth start one thought at a time—and you have the power to rewrite your story.

Chapter 9
Healing Betrayal

Betrayal Trauma: Healing the Wounds of Broken Trust

Betrayal trauma is one of the most painful emotional wounds you can experience. When someone you deeply trust—whether a spouse, close friend, family member, or mentor—violates that trust, the impact can feel shattering. Infidelity, deception, emotional neglect, or broken promises cut deep, leaving behind a profound sense of loss, self-doubt, and instability.

The pain of betrayal is not just emotional; it affects how you see yourself, how you engage with others, and even how you relate to the world. In its wake, you may struggle with emotional dysregulation, an inability to trust, or a feeling that your very identity has been shaken. But healing is possible. It requires understanding your trauma response, allowing yourself to grieve, learning how to rebuild trust, and ultimately embracing new beginnings.

Understanding the Trauma Response in Betrayal

Imagine your brain as a finely tuned instrument, calibrated to the rhythm of trust and connection. When betrayal strikes, it throws everything into disarray, much like an orchestra suddenly losing its conductor. Confusion, emotional chaos, and a sense of danger take over, making it feel as if the ground beneath you has been pulled away.

At the core of this reaction is your brain's survival system. Betrayal trauma activates the amygdala (the brain's fear center), triggering a heightened state of alertness and emotional reactivity. When this happens, rational thought takes a backseat, and your body enters fight, flight, freeze, or fawn mode—leading to overwhelming emotions, fear, and deep insecurity. Even when there is no immediate threat, your nervous system remains on high alert, scanning for danger in ways that can feel exhausting and uncontrollable.

For those who have experienced deep betrayal—whether in the form of infidelity, deception, emotional neglect, or broken promises—the emotional fallout can be devastating. Your brain struggles to make sense of the violation of trust, and in doing so, it often triggers responses that are difficult to regulate.

If you find yourself stuck in cycles of hypervigilance, distrust, or emotional overwhelm, know that these responses are not a sign of weakness—they are your brain's way of trying to protect you from further harm. Healing from betrayal trauma is not about forgetting what happened; it's about learning how to process, regulate, and rebuild—so that your past no longer dictates your future.

Common Trauma Responses to Betrayal

> ***Hypervigilance*** – The betrayed individual often becomes hyper-alert, scanning for signs of deception or abandonment. It's as if every

conversation, every pause in a text message, every shift in tone could be a potential threat. This can lead to **constant suspicion, anxiety, and overanalyzing interactions**, making it difficult to feel safe even in relationships that remain intact.

Emotional Flooding – Picture a dam breaking—anger, grief, shame, and sadness crash together, making it nearly impossible to think clearly. It can feel like you're drowning in emotions, unable to regain balance. In this state, even small triggers—like seeing a happy couple walking hand in hand or hearing a familiar song—can reopen the emotional wound, making it feel as if the betrayal just happened.

Identity Shattering – Trust forms the **bedrock of our self-worth**. When that trust is broken, it can feel as though the very foundation of who we are has fractured. Many people in the wake of betrayal question their judgment, wondering, *How did I not see this coming? Am I even the person I thought I was?* Self-doubt takes hold, and a sense of personal failure can cloud the ability to move forward.

Melissa's Story: A Personal Example

Consider Melissa, who discovered that her husband had been emotionally unfaithful. The revelation turned her world upside down. Once confident and secure, she found herself second-guessing everything—from her memories of their relationship to her ability to read people. She experienced intense mood swings, ranging from rage to deep sadness. Everyday moments—like seeing a couple laughing together at a café—became triggers for grief and suspicion. Conversations with her husband became interrogations, as every small action felt like another betrayal.

Melissa's story illustrates how deeply betrayal trauma can impact mental health, emotional stability, and one's sense of safety. It also shows that healing isn't just about time passing—it's about actively working through the emotional wreckage to reclaim a sense of trust, not just in others, but in oneself.

Accepting and Processing Your Emotions with Emotional Intelligence

One of the biggest barriers to healing is **emotional resistance**—the belief that certain emotions are "wrong" or that we should suppress them. But emotional health isn't about eliminating pain; it's about learning to **sit with it, understand it, and move through it**.

Healing from betrayal begins with *emotional intelligence*—the ability to recognize, understand, and regulate emotions. Without this awareness, emotions can feel chaotic and overpowering. But when we allow ourselves to truly process emotions rather than resist them, we take back control of our inner world.

How to Process Emotions Instead of Resisting Them

- Acknowledge What You Feel Without Judgment – Instead of labeling emotions as good or bad, recognize them as signals from your inner world. Saying I feel abandoned is different from I am unworthy. The first acknowledges a feeling; the second reinforces a false belief.

- Ask Yourself What This Emotion Is Teaching You – Every emotion holds valuable insight. Is your anger revealing an unmet need? Is your sadness signaling that something requires healing? Treat your emotions as messengers rather than enemies.
- Allow the Emotion to Run Its Course – Studies show that an emotional reaction, when not fueled by resistance, lasts approximately 90 seconds. When you allow yourself to fully experience an emotion rather than fight it, it naturally begins to dissipate. The goal is not to suppress it but to let it move through you.

David's Emotional Breakthrough

David had spent years pushing down grief after his divorce, refusing to acknowledge the depth of his pain. Anytime emotions surfaced, he distracted himself with work or numbed the pain with alcohol. But one night, he decided to try something different. Instead of resisting the sadness, he allowed himself to sit with it.

He sat quietly, breathed through the discomfort, and asked himself, *"What is this sadness trying to tell me?"*

For the first time, he realized his pain wasn't just about the loss of his marriage—it was about feeling unworthy of love. This realization changed everything. Instead of running from his emotions, he started working with them, leading to deep healing.

Reflection Exercise: Facing Your Own Emotions

Have you been resisting any emotions lately? What might happen if you allowed yourself to fully feel and process them?

- Take a few moments to reflect:
- What emotions have you been avoiding?
- How have you been numbing, suppressing, or ignoring them?
- What would it look like to sit with your emotions instead of running from them?

Write down your thoughts in a journal. Acknowledging emotions is the first step toward healing.

Seeking Safe Support Networks

Isolation magnifies pain. When betrayal occurs, the instinct for many is to withdraw—either out of shame, exhaustion, or a belief that no one will understand. However, healing happens in safe spaces, surrounded by people who can hold space for your emotions without judgment.

Seeking trusted friends, a therapist, or a support group provides a safe space to process emotions. Sharing your story with people who validate your pain rather than dismiss it is essential for healing.

If you struggle with trusting others after betrayal, start small. Open up to one safe person, even if it's just sharing a little of what you're feeling. You don't have to carry this alone.

Biblical Insight: God's Comfort in Betrayal

"The Lord is close to the brokenhearted and saves those who are crushed in spirit." (Psalm 34:18)

Even in our deepest wounds, we are not alone. Healing is possible, and God walks with us in our grief. Trust that, even when it feels impossible, there is a path forward.

Envisioning a New Life Beyond Betrayal

It's easy to assume that life will always be defined by pain or trauma, but this is not the final chapter of your story. What if, instead of assuming the worst, you imagined multiple possible futures for yourself—ones where healing, peace, and even joy are possible?

Envision:

- A version of yourself free from the weight of betrayal, no longer defined by what happened.
- A life where you trust again—not blindly, but wisely, with discernment and strength.
- A future where you feel whole, even if the road to healing is still unfolding.

Betrayal does not define you. What you choose to do next often does.

Your Next Step: Moving Forward

- Identify one emotion you've been resisting and allow yourself to feel it today.
- Reach out to one trusted person for support—someone who will listen without judgment.

- Journal about what your healing journey could look like. What would your life be like if betrayal no longer had power over you?

Remember: You are not broken—you are simply healing one step at a time.

Grieving the Past to Move Toward the Future

Healing from betrayal requires grief. Many people try to bypass the grieving process, hoping that if they ignore the pain, it will fade on its own. But unresolved pain never truly disappears—it simply manifests in other ways: through anger, emotional numbness, avoidance, or even self-destructive behaviors.

Suppressing emotions may seem like a form of control, but in reality, it prolongs suffering. To truly move forward, we must first allow ourselves to mourn what was lost—the relationship, the trust, the future we once envisioned.

Key Steps in the Grieving Process

- Allow Yourself to Feel Without Judgment. Grief is not a weakness—it is a natural response to loss. Give yourself permission to feel the full range of emotions—the anger, the sorrow, the confusion. You do not need to "be strong" by pretending you are unaffected. Cry if you need to. Let the emotions surface. Healing begins when you stop resisting what is already there.
- Write a Goodbye Letter. One of the most powerful ways to process betrayal is to write a letter to the person who hurt you. You don't have to send it—this is for your healing, not theirs. Express everything you need to

say: the pain, the questions, the disappointment. Then, in your own time, decide how you want to release it—whether by tearing it up, burning it, or simply storing it away.
- Practice Self-Compassion. Betrayal often brings self-doubt. Many people find themselves asking:

"Was I not enough?"

"Did I deserve this?"

"Should I have seen this coming?"

But betrayal is not a reflection of your worth. Someone else's choices do not define you. Remind yourself:

> "I am not responsible for another person's actions. I am worthy of love, honesty, and respect."

Envisioning a New Story Beyond the Trauma

When we are in pain, it's easy to believe that life will always be painful. Trauma narrows our vision, making it feel as though suffering is permanent. But healing requires us to reclaim the narrative—to imagine multiple possibilities for the future rather than assuming our past will define us forever.

How to Create a New Vision for Your Future

- Challenge the "This Is How It Will Always Be" Mentality
- Pain is part of your story, but it is not the whole story. Instead of assuming your life will always be marked by this betrayal, ask yourself:

"What if, five years from now, my life looks completely different? What if this season of healing leads to something greater than I imagined?"

- Write Down Multiple Scenarios for the Future
- Instead of seeing only one path forward, try envisioning different possibilities. Write down at least three different ways your future could unfold, such as:
- Scenario 1: "In two years, I am thriving in a new relationship, having learned to trust again."
- Scenario 2: "I have built a fulfilling single life, traveling and deepening my friendships."
- Scenario 3: "I have turned my pain into purpose, mentoring others who have gone through betrayal."

There is no single 'right' way to heal. What matters is that you allow yourself to imagine a future that is not controlled by your past wounds.

Sarah's Decision to Rewrite Her Story

Sarah spent years feeling trapped in a victim mindset after being abandoned by her fiancé. Every day, she told herself the same painful story:

> "I was left. I am unworthy. I will never trust again."

But one day, she asked herself, What if this is just one chapter, not the whole book?

She began visualizing new possibilities—what if she found a deeper love, not just in romance but in friendships and purpose? What if she used this season of singleness to explore passions she had ignored?

By choosing to believe in multiple outcomes, Sarah stopped defining herself by her past and started moving toward her future.

Reflection:

- What story have you been telling yourself about your future?
- What alternative possibilities can you envision instead?

Write down three potential futures for yourself—without limiting yourself to what you think is "realistic."

Biblical Insight: Trusting in a Future Beyond Pain

"For I know the plans I have for you," declares the Lord, "plans to prosper you and not to harm you, plans to give you hope and a future." (Jeremiah 29:11)

This scripture reminds us that pain is not the end of our story. God's plan includes restoration, renewal, and hope. The challenge is to trust in the process, even when we can't yet see the full picture.

Navigating the Path to Forgiveness

Forgiveness is often misunderstood. It is not about excusing betrayal or pretending the pain doesn't exist. Instead, it's about releasing its hold on you.

Forgiveness is not for the betrayer—it is for you. Holding onto resentment keeps you emotionally tied to the person who hurt you. Letting go is an act of self-liberation.

Psychological Explanation of Forgiveness

- Forgiveness ≠ Forgetting – Many people resist forgiveness because they think it means erasing the past. But forgiveness does not mean you excuse what happened; it means you refuse to let it define your future.
- The Role of Empathy – While difficult, understanding why someone acted as they did can help ease resentment. This does not mean justifying their behavior, but it can lessen the emotional grip their actions have over you.

Sarah's Story: Learning to Let Go

After being betrayed by her best friend, Sarah carried years of anger. She replayed the betrayal over and over in her mind, allowing resentment to shape her worldview.

One day, she decided to start journaling about her emotions. Writing allowed her to process her pain, rather than suppress it. Over time, she realized that forgiveness wasn't about reconciling with her friend—it was about freeing herself from the bitterness that was weighing her down.

Therapeutic Strategies for Forgiveness

- Journaling Your Feelings – Putting emotions into words helps clarify thoughts and release built-up pain.
- Practicing Empathy – This doesn't mean excusing someone's actions, but recognizing their human flaws can make it easier to let go.

- Setting Boundaries – Forgiveness does not mean allowing someone to hurt you again. Boundaries protect your peace while still allowing you to move forward.

Biblical Insight: Forgiveness as Liberation

"For if you forgive other people when they sin against you, your heavenly Father will also forgive you." (Matthew 6:14)

Forgiveness is not weakness—it is strength. It is a gift you give yourself, a release from the weight of resentment.

Your Next Steps: Moving Forward

- Write a "goodbye letter" or a "forgiveness letter" to the person who betrayed you (you don't have to send it).
- Identify one false belief you've been carrying since the betrayal (e.g., I am unworthy of love). Replace it with a new, empowering belief.
- Choose one way to envision a new future—write it down, create a vision board, or pray over it.

Reclaiming Your Story

- Betrayal is not the final word in your life.
- You have the power to heal.
- You are not the pain you experienced.
- You are not the actions of others.
- You are resilient, worthy, and capable of rebuilding a future full of love, trust, and joy.

What story will you choose to tell yourself moving forward?

Embracing New Beginnings After Betrayal

Betrayal often feels like an ending—an unraveling of the life you once knew. But what if, instead of being the final chapter, this moment became the catalyst for something greater? While the pain is real and valid, it also holds within it an undeniable opportunity for transformation.

Many who have walked through betrayal find that it leads them to strengths they never knew they had, dreams they had long abandoned, and a sense of self that is no longer dependent on others' actions. The choice is not whether betrayal will change you—it already has. The choice is how it will change you. Will it leave you bitter, or will it refine you into someone wiser, more resilient, and more whole?

The Psychology of Growth After Betrayal

Pain, when processed intentionally, can be a teacher. While betrayal shakes your sense of safety, it also forces you to examine your core beliefs, boundaries, and desires. If navigated with intention, this process can lead to profound personal growth.

Adopting a Growth Mindset

A *growth mindset* is the belief that challenges—no matter how painful—are opportunities for development. It shifts your perspective from *Why did this happen to me?* to *What can this experience teach me?* Instead of defining yourself by what happened, you begin defining yourself by how you **rise** from it.

Resilience Building. Each intentional step toward healing strengthens your ability to navigate future challenges with wisdom and strength. Emotional resilience isn't about avoiding pain but about learning how to recover from it more quickly.

Reclaiming Your Personal Power. Betrayal often leaves people feeling powerless. Rebuilding your life—whether through setting new goals, strengthening your identity, or reclaiming your independence—restores your sense of control.

Lisa's Story: Turning Betrayal into Opportunity

Lisa spent years building a business alongside someone she trusted completely. When her business partner secretly diverted clients and resources for personal gain, she was left devastated—not just financially, but emotionally. She questioned her judgment, lost confidence in herself, and struggled with feelings of betrayal that seeped into every area of her life.

For months, Lisa felt stuck in rage and self-doubt. But one day, she asked herself a simple but profound question: *If I could build a company once, why can't I do it again—on my own terms?*

With that shift in perspective, Lisa decided to rebuild. She launched her own business, implementing the lessons learned from her betrayal—stronger contracts, clearer boundaries, and a deeper trust in her own instincts. Over time, she not only thrived professionally but also discovered a newfound sense of confidence, resilience, and purpose.

Betrayal did change Lisa—but instead of letting it define her in despair, she used it as fuel to create a life she had once been too afraid to pursue.

Your Journey of Healing and Growth

The same power that Lisa discovered exists within you. Healing from betrayal is not just about moving on from what was lost—it's about rebuilding something even stronger in its place.

To begin this journey, consider taking these steps:

- Identify One Emotional Trigger Related to Betrayal. What situations or thoughts immediately bring up pain from the betrayal? Once you've identified a trigger, choose one grounding technique to help you navigate it—whether it's deep breathing, reciting a mantra, or engaging in a calming activity.
- Set Aside Time to Grieve. Healing cannot happen if pain is buried. Make space to grieve the past—whether through journaling, prayer, therapy, or creative expression. Let yourself release the emotions rather than suppress them.
- Rebuild Trust—Starting with Yourself. Many people assume that healing from betrayal is about learning to trust others again. But the real work begins with rebuilding trust in yourself—in your own intuition, decisions, and resilience. Start by making and keeping small personal commitments each day, proving to yourself that you are reliable and capable.

Biblical Insight: A Future Beyond Betrayal

> "Forget the former things; do not dwell on the past. See, I am doing a new thing!" (Isaiah 43:18-19)

God's plan for your life did not end with betrayal. The pain you feel today is not the conclusion—it is simply a chapter in your story. A new beginning is unfolding, even if you cannot yet see it.

Healing is not about rushing to "move on" or pretending the pain never happened. It's about learning, growing, and trusting that the future holds something greater.

Take the first step today. You are not just surviving betrayal—you are rising from it.

Chapter 10
Building Resilience

Building Emotional Resilience Through Faith

Healing from emotional dysregulation is not merely a psychological or relational process—it is also a deeply spiritual journey. Your faith offers a framework for understanding suffering, finding meaning in pain, and developing the resilience needed to face life's challenges. It transforms healing from a battle of self-reliance into an act of surrender, where divine restoration becomes the foundation for emotional stability.

Yet, in moments of emotional overwhelm, integrating faith into your healing can feel distant or even unfamiliar. You may wonder: *How does trusting in God help regulate emotions? What role does faith play when the pain feels insurmountable?* These are not abstract questions—they are the lived experience of countless individuals who have walked this road before you.

Faith as an Anchor in Emotional Healing

John had always struggled with emotional outbursts. His temper flared easily, and his relationships bore the weight of his unresolved pain. For years, he tried to manage his emotions through sheer willpower, but nothing changed. Then he turned to scripture. He began reading Psalms each day and meditating on its words. Over time, something shifted. Instead of reacting impulsively to frustration, he started bringing his emotions to God—pausing, praying, and allowing divine wisdom to shape his response.

Faith, as John discovered, is more than belief—it's a stabilizing force that can help restructure emotional responses. Research supports this. Individuals with a strong faith often experience lower levels of stress and depression, in part because their sense of purpose extends beyond immediate circumstances. Prayer and meditation—core spiritual practices—have been shown to activate the parasympathetic nervous system, which helps the body return to a state of calm.

In this way, faith is not just a source of spiritual comfort—it's also a physiological tool for regulating your emotions.

But perhaps more importantly, faith provides something essential for healing: hope. When trauma shakes your emotional world, hope becomes an anchor, grounding you in the truth that restoration is possible. In the unpredictable waters of emotional dysregulation, faith is the lighthouse that keeps you steady.

Faith-Based Journaling: Inviting God into Your Healing Journey

Melissa had never considered journaling to be a spiritual practice. To her, it was just something people did to document their days. But after a painful season of betrayal and loss, she found herself sitting with a journal, pen in hand, overwhelmed with questions: *Why did this happen? Where is God in my pain? How do I move forward?*

At first, her journal entries were raw—filled with anger, grief, and confusion. But as time went on, her writing became a conversation with God. Her entries turned into written prayers, moments of surrender, and eventually, signs of healing. She realized she wasn't just venting—she was opening her heart to divine presence.

Faith-based journaling invites God into your healing process. Writing down your thoughts, prayers, struggles, and insights creates a sacred space for reflection and restoration. Whether you're pouring out pain in a letter to God, tracking answered prayers, or meditating on scripture, this practice transforms your inner turmoil into a dialogue—one that leads to healing rather than isolation.

Shifting Perspective Through Gratitude

When you're in the depths of emotional pain, it's easy to focus only on what's missing, broken, or lost. But gratitude has the power to shift your perspective. It doesn't deny your suffering—it simply reminds you that light still exists, even in the darkest places.

Emily started a simple practice. Each morning, before checking her phone, she wrote down three things she was grateful for. Some days, it was something small—the warmth of coffee, the way the sun filtered through her window. Other days, it was a kind word, a moment of peace, or a scripture verse that touched her heart. Slowly, her emotions began to shift. Grief and sorrow didn't disappear—but they no longer had the final say. Joy began to reenter her life, one grateful moment at a time.

Gratitude is a spiritual discipline that retrains your mind to look beyond present pain. Scripture affirms this posture: *"Give thanks in all circumstances; for this is God's will for you in Christ Jesus"* (1 Thessalonians 5:18). Gratitude doesn't mean pretending everything is fine—it means choosing to see that God's grace is still present, even when healing is still unfolding.

Faith, Healing, and the Journey Ahead

Emotional healing is not a straight line. It's a journey of relearning, rebuilding, and remembering who you are—not just as someone recovering from pain, but as someone deeply loved and guided by a faithful God.

Through faith, you're invited into a deeper kind of healing—one that embraces your full humanity and welcomes divine restoration. Let your faith be your compass. Let prayer be your breath. Let scripture be your anchor. And in every moment—especially the hard ones—trust that you are not walking alone.

The Power of Forgiveness in Emotional Healing

Betrayal had left Sarah bitter, her heart hardened by years of unresolved pain. She carried the weight of anger like a shield, believing that holding onto it protected her from being hurt again. But the reality was far different—her resentment did not safeguard her; it imprisoned her.

Forgiveness, she learned, was not about minimizing the betrayal or excusing what had happened. It was about releasing the power that pain had over her. Through prayer and self-reflection, she made the difficult choice to forgive—not for the sake of the person who wronged her, but for her own freedom.

Unforgiveness keeps the body in a heightened state of stress, triggering chronic anxiety and even physical ailments. It creates a cycle of emotional reactivity, where the past dictates the present. But grace interrupts this cycle. Choosing forgiveness—whether for others or for oneself—opens the door to emotional stability.

For those struggling to forgive, the process may begin with small steps: writing an unsent letter to the person who caused harm, praying for the strength to let go of resentment, or practicing self-compassion by releasing personal guilt. Scripture offers wisdom in this process: "Be kind to one another, tenderhearted, forgiving one another, as God in Christ forgave you" (Ephesians 4:32). Forgiveness is not a one-time act but a journey—one that leads to peace.

Trusting God for Inner Transformation

David's past was marked by emotional neglect, leaving him desperate for control. He read every self-help book he could find, attended therapy, and meticulously planned his healing journey, hoping to fast-track the process. Yet peace remained elusive. It wasn't until he surrendered—truly surrendered—his pain to God that healing began to take root.

Letting go of control is one of the hardest aspects of emotional healing. The mind craves certainty, solutions, and immediate relief. But transformation is not something that can be forced—it unfolds in God's timing. Trusting in

His plan allows for acceptance, patience, and resilience rather than frustration and fear.

David found solace in daily prayers of surrender. Each morning, he committed his struggles to God, releasing his need for control. He memorized verses about God's faithfulness, allowing scripture to reshape his thinking. He joined a faith-based support group, finding strength in community rather than isolation. In time, he realized that healing was not about achieving a perfect emotional state but about learning to trust, even in the unknown.

Scripture reinforces this truth: "Trust in the Lord with all your heart, and do not lean on your own understanding" (Proverbs 3:5). Emotional resilience is not built on self-reliance—it is forged in surrender.

Applying These Lessons: Taking the First Step

Healing is an ongoing process—one that requires faith, forgiveness, and trust. As you move forward in your own journey, consider what steps you can take today.

Are there areas of your life where you need to practice gratitude, even in hardship? Can you begin releasing resentment by writing a forgiveness letter, even if you never send it? What would it look like to surrender control and trust God's plan instead of striving for immediate answers?

Faith provides the foundation for emotional resilience, offering hope in the midst of struggle. Forgiveness releases the chains of the past, allowing peace to take its place. Trust in God transforms healing from a battle into a journey of renewal.

Healing is not about reaching a destination. It is about walking forward, step by step, with faith as your guide.

The Process of Reclaiming Rational Thought

As David delved deeper into his healing, he encountered one of the most formidable challenges yet: emotional dysregulation clouded his ability to think clearly. Time and time again, he found himself reacting impulsively, making rash decisions, and struggling to engage in rational conversations. It felt as though emotions had hijacked his reasoning, pulling him into a whirlwind of overreactions and misinterpretations.

But as healing took root, something remarkable happened—his ability to engage with reality in a healthier and more balanced way returned. Rational thought was not lost forever; it had simply been buried beneath years of unresolved pain. This chapter explores the journey of regaining logical engagement, overcoming emotional rigidity, and developing the cognitive flexibility essential for both personal and relational growth.

How Emotional Healing Restores Clarity and Reason

Understanding the connection between emotional regulation and rational thinking requires looking at how the brain processes overwhelming emotions. When emotions run high, the amygdala—the brain's fear and emotion center—dominates, overpowering the prefrontal cortex, which is responsible for logical reasoning. This means that in moments of intense distress, emotions become the sole driver of thoughts and behaviors, leading to impulsive decisions and distorted interpretations of reality.

As the healing process unfolds, the brain begins to rebalance:

- The prefrontal cortex regains strength, allowing logical thinking to take precedence.
- Emotional reactivity decreases, creating space for thoughtful, measured responses.
- Individuals learn to discern between emotional impulses and objective reality, leading to healthier interactions and decision-making.

Maria's story illustrates this transformation. Carrying the weight of abandonment trauma, she often reacted intensely to simple disappointments. If a friend canceled plans, she automatically assumed she was being rejected. This assumption sent her into spirals of distress, reinforcing a narrative of unworthiness. However, after months of therapy and self-reflection, she developed the ability to pause and assess situations objectively. She began to ask herself, *What else could this mean?* Instead of assuming rejection, she considered alternative explanations—maybe her friend had an unexpected obligation or needed rest. This shift allowed her to break free from emotional assumptions and engage with reality from a place of clarity.

Developing Cognitive Flexibility After Emotional Rigidity

Cognitive flexibility—the ability to shift perspectives, consider multiple viewpoints, and adapt to new information—is essential for problem-solving, conflict resolution, and emotional stability. However, for individuals with a history of trauma, cognitive rigidity often takes hold, making it difficult to see beyond black-and-white thinking.

Mark, for instance, had spent years viewing relationships through a lens of deep suspicion. His past betrayals had conditioned him to believe that no one could be trusted. This belief, though understandable, became a roadblock in his healing. Every new relationship was met with skepticism, and he often misinterpreted neutral behaviors as potential threats.

As Mark progressed in his healing journey, he slowly began to challenge these rigid thought patterns. He realized that not everyone was a reflection of his past pain and that trust could be rebuilt, albeit with discernment and patience. This shift required intentional practice:

- Instead of immediately assuming deception, he paused and asked, What else could be true?
- He actively engaged in discussions with people he trusted, exposing himself to differing viewpoints without defensiveness.
- He kept a journal, tracking moments when his rigid thoughts arose and working to challenge them in real time.

Over time, cognitive flexibility became second nature, allowing him to navigate relationships with greater openness and trust.

The Stages of Healing That Restore Rational Thought

Healing from emotional dysregulation is a process that unfolds in stages. Much like rebuilding physical strength after an injury, each step contributes to emotional resilience and a more balanced engagement with the world.

Stage 1: Emotional Awareness

The journey begins with recognizing emotional triggers—the moments that send emotions spiraling out of control. This awareness is the first step in regaining rational engagement. Are there recurring themes in your reactions? Do conflicts with loved ones repeatedly stir up the same feelings? Identifying these patterns provides valuable insight into what needs healing.

Personal reflection can be a powerful tool here. Consider writing down instances where emotions have overwhelmed your ability to think clearly. What happened? What were you feeling in that moment? The act of documenting these experiences brings them into the light, allowing you to begin processing them constructively.

Pausing before reacting also plays a vital role. Imagine standing at the edge of an emotional storm but choosing not to be swept away. Instead of immediately responding to a triggering event, take a deep breath and give yourself space to assess the situation objectively.

Stage 2: Emotional Regulation Skills

With awareness comes the need for regulation. Grounding techniques serve as a powerful tool to anchor yourself in the present moment. Whether it's focusing on your breath, using sensory grounding exercises, or engaging in a brief walk, these practices help diffuse emotional intensity.

Consider a scenario where you feel frustration building in a conversation. Instead of letting emotions dictate your response, you pause and take a slow breath, giving yourself the time to choose how you want to react. This simple yet intentional act can prevent unnecessary conflict and help maintain emotional stability.

Alongside grounding techniques, developing healthy coping mechanisms is essential. What activities bring you a sense of peace? Journaling, engaging in creative expression, or practicing gratitude can all serve as outlets for emotional processing. By integrating these practices into daily life, emotional regulation becomes a habit rather than a struggle.

Stage 3: Strengthening Rational Thought

Once emotional responses are managed, it becomes easier to engage in rational thought. Cognitive restructuring—challenging distorted thought patterns—is a crucial skill in this stage. Instead of falling into negative self-talk, practice reframing your thoughts.

For instance, if your immediate reaction to a mistake is, *I always mess things up,* shift it to, *I am learning and growing through experience.* This small but significant change rewires the brain, reinforcing a more constructive and realistic perspective.

Equally important is practicing rational discussion. Engaging in conversations with an open mind, without defensiveness, strengthens one's ability to communicate effectively. Imagine a disagreement where both parties feel heard and respected instead of resorting to emotional outbursts. This type of interaction is possible when rational engagement is prioritized.

Stage 4: Cognitive and Relational Flexibility

The final stage involves embracing flexibility—both in thinking and in relationships. This means being open to alternative viewpoints and engaging in discussions without feeling threatened.

Samantha had spent years reacting aggressively in arguments, convinced that her way was the only correct perspective. But as she worked through the stages of healing, she became less reactive, more measured in her responses, and better able to engage in discussions without escalating conflict. She learned to listen actively, seek understanding, and recognize that differing opinions were not personal attacks.

In moments of disagreement, stepping into the other person's perspective can lead to more productive and empathetic conversations. Rather than shutting down or lashing out, ask yourself, *How might they be seeing this situation differently?* This mindset shift fosters relational harmony and emotional growth.

Embracing the Journey Toward Rational Thought

Reclaiming rational thought is not about suppressing emotions—it's about integrating them with wisdom. Emotional healing does not erase feelings; rather, it brings balance between emotion and logic, allowing individuals to respond rather than react.

As you continue this journey, reflect on where you are in the process. Are there emotional triggers that still hold power over you? What strategies have helped you regain clarity? How can you practice cognitive flexibility in daily interactions?

Healing is not linear, and setbacks may come. But each step forward—each moment of awareness, each pause before reaction, each reframed thought—moves you closer to a life defined not by emotional chaos, but by thoughtful, intentional engagement with reality.

Recognizing When You Are Emotionally Dysregulated and Unfit for Serious Discussion

Engaging in meaningful conversations requires a level of emotional stability that allows for rational thought and mutual understanding. However, when emotions take over, discussions can quickly spiral into conflict, leaving both parties feeling unheard and misunderstood. Recognizing when you are emotionally dysregulated is essential for maintaining constructive communication and preventing unnecessary damage to relationships.

Understanding the Signs of Emotional Dysregulation

Imagine standing in the middle of an intense conversation, feeling your heart race and your mind struggle to form coherent thoughts. Instead of responding logically, you find yourself either withdrawing completely or reacting impulsively. This is emotional dysregulation in action—a state where emotions override reason, making productive discussions nearly impossible.

The most common signs of dysregulation include racing thoughts that make it difficult to follow logical arguments, emotional flooding that leads to defensiveness or irrational anger, and physical reactions such as a rapid heartbeat, muscle tension, or sweating. In these moments, continuing the conversation is often counterproductive.

Tom, for example, frequently found himself raising his voice in disagreements with his spouse, unable to control his frustration. However, once he learned to recognize the physical and emotional signs of dysregulation, he started pausing mid-conversation, saying, *"I need a moment to process."* This simple habit prevented escalation, allowing him to return to discussions with a clearer mind.

Stepping Away to Regain Composure

When you recognize the early signs of emotional overwhelm, stepping away from the discussion can be the most responsible and productive action. This doesn't mean avoiding difficult conversations, but rather ensuring that they take place when both parties are in a state of emotional balance. Pausing allows your nervous system to calm, preventing words spoken in frustration from causing lasting harm.

Grounding techniques can be particularly effective in these moments. Deep breathing exercises, such as inhaling for four counts, holding for four, and exhaling for four, can help reset the nervous system. Sensory-based grounding—like placing your feet firmly on the floor or running your hands under cool water—can also bring immediate relief.

Additionally, rescheduling the conversation for a later time, when emotions have settled, allows for more thoughtful and constructive dialogue. Rather than forcing yourself to continue when dysregulated, choosing to wait until you can engage with clarity is an act of emotional intelligence and self-awareness.

Biblical wisdom reinforces this principle: *"A gentle answer turns away wrath, but a harsh word stirs up anger."* (Proverbs 15:1). Recognizing when you are unfit for serious discussion and choosing to pause prevents unnecessary conflict, allowing grace and understanding to take the lead.

Cognitive Flexibility Must Be Developed Intentionally

Picture a tree swaying in the wind—its branches bending with the movement but never breaking. This image captures the essence of cognitive flexibility, the ability to adapt your thinking in response to new information, unexpected changes, or differing perspectives. Unlike rigid thought patterns that lead to frustration and conflict, cognitive flexibility allows for problem-solving, personal growth, and stronger relationships.

Developing this skill requires intentional effort. Many individuals instinctively hold onto their perspectives, unwilling to entertain alternative viewpoints. However, making a conscious decision to practice flexibility opens the door to deeper connections and greater emotional resilience.

Consider a situation where you and a friend disagree on weekend plans. Instead of rigidly insisting on your preference, take a step back and ask yourself, *What does my friend need right now?* This simple shift in mindset fosters compromise and mutual respect.

Another way to cultivate flexibility is by actively challenging automatic thoughts. If someone cancels on you, your immediate assumption might be, *They don't value our friendship.* Instead, pause and consider alternative explanations: *Maybe they're overwhelmed or dealing with personal stress.* By practicing this habit daily, you train your brain to move away from rigid thinking and toward a more balanced, rational approach.

Recognizing Dysregulation Prevents Unnecessary Conflict

Uncontrolled emotions can turn minor disagreements into major disputes. Recognizing when you are dysregulated allows you to take proactive steps before a conversation becomes unproductive or hurtful. Imagine being in a heated discussion, and suddenly, you notice your pulse quicken, your muscles tense, and your thoughts race. These are signals from your body urging you to pause and regain control.

Instead of reacting impulsively, stepping back allows for self-reflection. In that moment, ask yourself: *Am I responding to the present situation, or am I carrying emotional weight from the past?* By slowing down and acknowledging what's happening internally, you create the space to choose a more measured response.

Tracking emotional patterns through journaling can also provide valuable insights. Documenting when dysregulation occurs and the emotions tied to it helps reveal triggers, making it easier to develop strategies for managing them in the future.

Tracking Progress in Rational Engagement

Rational engagement is not just about clear communication; it's about fostering connection and understanding. As you work on strengthening this skill, tracking your progress can be a powerful motivator. Reflect on recent conversations—what strategies helped you stay composed? Did you actively listen? Were you able to express yourself without defensiveness?

Keeping a *discussion journal* can be particularly helpful. At the end of each week, write down highlights from conversations where you felt engaged and in control. Note what worked well and what could be improved. Over time, this practice reinforces positive habits and reveals areas for continued growth.

Start by setting small, achievable goals. If you tend to interrupt when emotions rise, challenge yourself to pause and fully listen before responding. If you often assume the worst in conflicts, practice reframing situations by considering multiple perspectives. Each effort, no matter how small, contributes to long-term emotional resilience.

Daily Cognitive Flexibility Exercise: A Path to Rational Thought

Imagine starting each day with the mindset that new perspectives and possibilities are waiting to be discovered. Cognitive flexibility is not just about handling conflicts—it's about embracing life with curiosity and openness.

One practical exercise to strengthen this skill is *seeking alternative explanations*. Throughout your day, whenever you encounter a frustrating situation, pause and consider at least three possible reasons for it. For instance, if a colleague seems distant in a meeting, instead of assuming they are upset with you, consider:

- They might be preoccupied with a personal issue.
- They could be exhausted from a demanding workload.
- They may be dealing with anxiety that has nothing to do with you.

By training yourself to challenge assumptions and embrace different viewpoints, you cultivate a mindset that fosters growth, empathy, and rational thinking.

Identifying Personal Dysregulation: Your Emotional Compass

Everyone experiences moments of emotional overwhelm, but recognizing these moments as they happen is what allows for intentional regulation. The body often signals distress before the mind fully registers it. Physical signs such as rapid heartbeat, tightness in the chest, or feeling on edge are cues that emotions are taking the lead.

When you become aware of these signs, take a step back. Identify the emotion—whether it's frustration, sadness, or fear—and acknowledge it without judgment. What triggered this reaction? What past experiences might be influencing your response? By developing this awareness, you gain the ability to manage emotions effectively rather than being controlled by them.

Applying These Lessons

Healing and emotional growth are ongoing processes that require patience and intentional practice. As you navigate your own journey, consider these daily practices to reinforce emotional stability and rational engagement:

- Keep a journal to track emotional triggers and reflect on patterns over time.
- Develop a personal grounding toolkit with strategies such as deep breathing, visualization, or taking a brief walk.
- Practice reframing negative thoughts by actively challenging automatic assumptions and considering alternative explanations.
- Recognize the signs of dysregulation and implement calming strategies before engaging in difficult conversations.

By incorporating these habits into your daily routine, you build a foundation of emotional resilience, allowing you to engage in meaningful discussions with clarity, wisdom, and self-awareness. Each step you take is an investment in your ability to navigate life's complexities with strength and grace.

Part 4
Maintaining Healthy Relationships

Chapter 11 Beyond Survival

Chapter 12 Trust in Marriage

Chapter 13 Loving the Dysregulated

Chapter 14 Trust in Parenting

Chapter 15 An Emotionally Regulated Family

Chapter 11
Beyond Survival

From Coping to Thriving: Embracing Emotional Wholeness

Healing from emotional dysregulation is not merely about avoiding emotional outbursts—it is about rediscovering joy, building stability, and cultivating fulfilling relationships. If you've spent years in survival mode, you may struggle to feel a deep sense of peace or connection. Your nervous system, conditioned to expect stress, unpredictability, or chaos, may even resist the very things that bring healing: rest, happiness, and trust in others.

This resistance is not a personal flaw—it's a survival adaptation. When emotional volatility has been your norm, calm can feel unfamiliar. When betrayal or disappointment has shaped your view of others, trust can feel unsafe. Yet, healing invites you to take the risk of stepping into something new: thriving, not just surviving.

This chapter explores how to make that transition. You'll learn how to move beyond coping mechanisms and step into a life marked by emotional clarity, internal peace, and meaningful connection. You'll be invited to embrace emotional wholeness—not as a destination you must reach perfectly, but as a lifelong journey of integration and restoration.

As you continue forward, know this: you were not created to live in a constant state of emotional reactivity. You were made for joy, stability, and love. And every step you take toward healing is a step closer to living that truth.

Learning to Live Beyond Survival Mode

What Is Survival Mode? Imagine waking up each day with a sense of impending doom, as if an invisible weight is pressing down on your chest. This is the essence of survival mode—a state of chronic stress where your brain is laser-focused on immediate safety and emotional reactivity. In survival mode, you're not thinking about growth or long-term goals. You're simply trying to make it through the next moment, often without realizing it.

In this state, the parts of your brain responsible for rational thought, empathy, and emotional regulation take a backseat to your body's threat detection system. The fight, flight, freeze, or fawn responses are constantly activated, keeping your nervous system on high alert.

While the human brain is brilliantly designed to protect you from real danger, it can become over-conditioned by past trauma, prolonged stress, or unresolved emotional pain. When survival mode becomes your default setting, it distorts your perception of reality—making even safe or neutral situations feel threatening.

Moments of calm may feel unfamiliar or even unsafe because your nervous system is used to chaos. Trust can feel dangerous. Joy might trigger suspicion. Rest can be uncomfortable. And instead of embracing peace, you may find yourself bracing for the next emotional storm.

Living in survival mode isn't just exhausting—it also blocks your ability to connect, create, and experience true joy. But the good news is this: survival mode is not permanent. With awareness, regulation, and healing, you can begin to rewire your nervous system, shift out of reactivity, and step into a life of safety, purpose, and emotional freedom.

Psychological Explanation of Survival Mode

- Hypervigilance & Emotional Exhaustion – Living in survival mode keeps the brain in a constant state of alertness. It becomes difficult to relax, trust, or enjoy the present moment because the mind is always scanning for the next threat. Over time, this leads to emotional and physical exhaustion.
- Fear-Based Decision-Making – When the brain is wired for survival, decisions are made out of fear rather than wisdom. Individuals in survival mode prioritize short-term emotional relief over long-term stability, making it hard to form healthy relationships or set meaningful goals.
- Limited Capacity for Joy – When stress becomes the baseline, happiness feels foreign or even unsafe. The brain, trained to expect turmoil, resists positive emotions, leading individuals to sabotage joyful experiences because they feel too vulnerable or unfamiliar.

Jake's Story: Always Bracing for Conflict

Jake grew up in a volatile home where peace never lasted long. He learned to be hyper-aware of small changes in tone, facial expressions, or body language, always anticipating the next argument. Even in his adult relationships, when things were calm, he couldn't enjoy the peace—his brain told him something bad was coming.

His wife, Emily, often reassured him that things were fine, but Jake's nervous system didn't believe it. He would pick fights, withdraw emotionally, or question his relationships—not because anything was wrong, but because his past had wired him to expect instability.

Jake's story highlights the pain of survival mode—even when life is safe, the body refuses to let go of old fears.

How to Transition from Surviving to Thriving

Breaking free from survival mode is possible, but it requires intentional effort to retrain the nervous system. The following practices help shift the brain from constant fear to a place of safety, balance, and joy.

Rewiring the Brain for Peace

Imagine stepping into a quiet, peaceful space, away from the noise and distractions of life. This is the essence of mindfulness. It is the practice of being present, fully engaged in the moment, without anticipating danger or catastrophe.

When individuals in survival mode practice mindfulness, they teach their nervous systems that it is safe to slow down. Over time, the brain rewires itself, moving away from automatic fear responses and toward calm, intentional awareness.

Practical Ways to Practice Mindfulness

- Pause and Breathe – Take five deep breaths when stress arises. Let your body register the fact that you are not in danger.
- Engage Your Senses – When anxiety spikes, focus on what you can see, hear, touch, and smell to ground yourself in the present moment.
- Slow Down Daily Tasks – Instead of rushing, try eating a meal, drinking tea, or taking a shower with full awareness, paying attention to every detail.

At first, mindfulness may feel uncomfortable—survival mode tells the brain that stillness is unsafe. But over time, this practice teaches the body that peace is possible.

Developing a Joy Routine

For many who have lived in survival mode, joy is not automatic—it must be intentionally cultivated. Imagine planting seeds in a garden; joy works the same way. The more you practice small moments of happiness, the easier it becomes to experience deep, lasting fulfillment.

How to Create a Joy Routine

- Reintroduce Playfulness – What activities made you feel alive as a child? Dancing? Painting? Exploring? Reconnect with past passions and allow yourself to engage in play without guilt.
- Schedule Moments of Joy – Set aside time each day for something you enjoy, whether it's listening to music, spending time in nature, or engaging in a creative hobby.

- Give Yourself Permission to Feel Happy – If you feel uneasy when joy arises, remind yourself: "I am allowed to enjoy this moment."

Just as survival mode takes time to unlearn, joy takes time to relearn. The more you prioritize small joys, the more your brain will begin to trust happiness again.

Practicing Gratitude: Shifting from Fear to Contentment

When stress and fear dominate life, it becomes easy to focus on what is missing or what could go wrong. Gratitude is the practice of redirecting attention toward what is good, stable, and fulfilling.

The Science of Gratitude

Studies show that daily gratitude rewires the brain, decreasing anxiety and increasing resilience. By intentionally shifting focus away from fear and toward appreciation, individuals retrain their emotional responses.

- Simple Ways to Practice Gratitude
- Write Down Three Good Things Each Day – They don't have to be big—even small moments of peace count.
- Express Gratitude to Others – Take a moment to thank a friend, partner, or family member for their presence in your life.
- Reflect on Past Growth – Remind yourself how far you've come. What challenges have you overcome? What lessons have you learned?

Gratitude does not mean ignoring pain or pretending everything is perfect. Instead, it is about acknowledging what is good, even in the midst of challenges.

Biblical Insight: Life Beyond Survival

> "I have come that they may have life, and have it to the full." (John 10:10)

This verse reminds us that we were not created merely to survive, but to thrive. Healing is not just about escaping pain—it is about embracing joy, peace, and emotional wholeness.

If you have spent years feeling trapped in survival mode, you are not alone. Healing is a process, but freedom is possible.

Begin Reclaiming Joy Today

This week, commit to one intentional step toward breaking free from survival mode. Choose one of the following and implement it into your daily life:

- Practice five minutes of mindfulness each morning.
- Schedule a small joy-filled activity just for yourself.
- Write down three things you are grateful for before bed.

As you begin integrating these practices, remind yourself: healing is not about returning to who you were before pain—it's about stepping into a new, thriving version of yourself.

Striving, Living, and Coping in the Real World

Embracing Emotional Wholeness

Healing is not simply about reducing distress—it is about reclaiming a life of emotional richness, balance, and connection. Too often, those who struggle with emotional dysregulation find themselves caught in cycles of either suppressing their emotions or being consumed by them. True healing happens when you learn to feel without being overwhelmed, express yourself without losing control, and respond rather than react. This is the essence of emotional wholeness.

Let's face it, just because you want to overcome the tyranny of emotional reasoning and arrested development or its other cousins, it's not going to be as simple as throwing a switch. Like all major life changes, it takes time and practice—lots of practice. And with practice comes some failures. So, it makes sense to begin by recognizing that there will be lapses, even relapses into old, failed strategies, conflicts, even fights. But with renewed effort, and armed with understanding and skills, you will overcome your lapses or find the fortitude to endure the relapses of your loved one. This section is about tolerating and coping. We will begin by examining the concept of emotional wholeness, as way to be okay with being present when unpleasant things are happening.

What Is Emotional Wholeness?

Emotional wholeness is the ability to be fully present with your emotions while maintaining stability. It doesn't mean avoiding pain or never feeling sadness, anger, or disappointment. Instead, it's about being in control of your emotions rather than being controlled by them.

Imagine standing in the ocean as waves roll in. Emotional dysregulation feels like being knocked down by every wave, struggling to stay afloat. Emotional wholeness, on the other hand, is learning to stand firm, letting the waves come and go without losing your balance.

Psychological Foundations of Emotional Wholeness

- Integrating Past Trauma – Emotional wholeness does not mean erasing the past. Instead, it means learning that your history informs you but does not control you. You acknowledge past wounds without allowing them to dictate your present reactions.
- Healthy Emotional Expression – Many struggle with two extremes: either suppressing their emotions or overreacting to them. True emotional health lies in the middle: processing emotions constructively, expressing them authentically, and releasing them without chaos.
- Balance Between Emotion and Logic – Emotionally whole individuals don't ignore their feelings, but they also don't allow emotions to override rational thought. They learn to acknowledge their feelings, evaluate them with wisdom, and respond thoughtfully.

As we journey through the complexities of healing, *reflect on your own emotional patterns.* How do you typically react to stress? Do you tend to shut down, lash out, or seek distractions? What small steps can you take to move from emotional survival into a life of stability, joy, and deep connection?

Emily's Story: From Emotional Extremes to Balance

Emily had spent most of her life oscillating between two extremes. At times, she shut down completely, avoiding emotions until they exploded uncontrollably. Other times, she was overcome by feelings of sadness, fear, or anger, reacting impulsively in ways she later regretted.

Through therapy and deep self-reflection, Emily discovered a powerful shift: she could validate her emotions without spiraling into chaos. She learned that feelings were not her enemy, nor were they absolute truth. They were simply signals, invitations to deeper understanding.

Her breakthrough came when she embraced three key strategies that helped her regulate emotions and reclaim control over her reactions.

Therapeutic Self-Help Strategies for Emotional Wholeness

1. Journaling for Emotional Processing

One of Emily's most profound discoveries was the power of journaling. Instead of reacting immediately when overwhelmed, she began to write down her thoughts and emotions first.

By putting words to her feelings, she was able to:

- Prevent emotional flooding, creating space between her emotions and her reactions.

- Recognize patterns in her triggers and responses.
- Gain clarity about whether her feelings were rooted in the present moment or unresolved past wounds.

How to Apply This Strategy: Try setting aside five minutes each evening to write about your day. What emotions surfaced? How did you handle them? What could you do differently next time?

2. Self-Compassion Exercises

For years, Emily had been her own harshest critic. Every mistake, every difficult emotion, and every perceived failure reinforced an internal dialogue of shame.

Through self-compassion practices, she learned to speak to herself with the same kindness she would offer a close friend. Instead of berating herself for feeling anxious or angry, she acknowledged her emotions with patience and grace.

How to Apply This Strategy: Next time you feel overwhelmed, pause and ask yourself, "If a dear friend were feeling this way, what would I say to them?" Then, offer yourself that same kindness.

3. The "Pause and Evaluate" Approach

One of Emily's most transformative habits was learning to *pause before reacting*. Instead of being immediately swept away by her emotions, she asked herself:

- "Is this feeling rooted in the present moment, or is it echoing past pain?"
- "What is the healthiest way to respond?"

- "What do I need right now to feel grounded?"

This simple act of pausing helped her disentangle old wounds from current situations. Over time, she noticed she was able to navigate emotions with far more clarity and control.

How to Apply This Strategy: Next time strong emotions arise, give yourself a 30-second pause before speaking or acting. Use this moment to assess what you truly need.

Biblical Insight: Healing and Restoration

> "He heals the brokenhearted and binds up their wounds." (Psalm 147:3)

This verse is a reminder that emotional healing is not something we must do alone. Just as physical wounds require care and time to heal, so do emotional wounds. Whether through therapy, community, or faith, healing is a process—a journey of restoration where old wounds no longer define us.

Your Next Steps Toward Emotional Wholeness

Healing is not about perfection; it is about progress. If you are committed to breaking free from emotional extremes and embracing balance, consider starting with one small, intentional step.

This week, choose one of the following:

- Write in a journal for five minutes each night. Reflect on your emotions and how you handled them.

- Practice self-compassion by replacing one self-critical thought with a kind and understanding one.
- Pause before reacting. When emotions rise, take a moment to assess whether your feelings are tied to the present moment or past wounds.

Each small action leads to profound transformation. The path to emotional wholeness is not about erasing difficult feelings but about learning to walk through them with stability, grace, and resilience.

How Emotional Regulation Enables Deeper Intellectual and Relational Clarity

The Link Between Emotional Regulation & Rational Thought

Emotional regulation is not just about maintaining inner peace—it directly impacts our ability to think clearly, engage with truth, and build strong relationships. When emotions are out of control, they hijack the brain's reasoning center, distorting perceptions and leading to impulsive reactions rather than thoughtful responses. However, when emotions are regulated, the mind becomes clear, allowing for deeper intellectual engagement and more fulfilling relational connections.

Imagine a world where your thoughts flow freely, unclouded by emotional turmoil. This is not an abstract ideal—it is the natural result of emotional regulation. When we achieve emotional stability, the prefrontal cortex—the part of our brain responsible for reasoning, decision-making, and problem-solving—functions optimally. This clarity is essential for engaging with truth, navigating complex issues, and understanding differing perspectives without defensiveness.

Psychological Foundations of Emotional Regulation and Rational Thinking

- Dysregulation Clouds Judgment – When emotions escalate, the brain's amygdala (the fear center) hijacks rational thinking. This leads to black-and-white thinking, preventing us from seeing the full picture.
- Regulation Promotes Open-Mindedness – Emotional stability allows us to process opposing viewpoints without feeling personally threatened. Instead of reacting defensively, we can engage in thoughtful discussions.
- Clarity Strengthens Relationships – Regulated emotions lead to better communication, conflict resolution, and deeper connections. When we are calm and self-aware, we can listen without projecting past wounds onto present conversations.

Mark's Story: From Reactivity to Rational Engagement

Mark had always struggled with defensiveness in conversations. If someone disagreed with him, he felt personally attacked. His emotional reactions turned minor disagreements into major conflicts, damaging both personal and professional relationships.

After working on emotional regulation techniques, Mark experienced a transformation. Instead of reacting impulsively, he learned to pause, reflect, and engage with clarity. He began to ask questions rather than assume intentions, allowing him to navigate discussions with wisdom rather than defensiveness.

His relationships improved dramatically—instead of arguing, he started listening. Instead of escalating conflicts, he resolved them. By regulating his emotions, he became a better thinker, communicator, and friend.

Therapeutic Self-Help Strategies for Enhancing Clarity Through Emotional Regulation

1. Pause Before Responding

One of Mark's most effective strategies was learning to pause before reacting. When emotions are high, the brain demands immediate action—but acting impulsively often leads to regret.

Instead of reacting instantly, he practiced:

- Taking three deep breaths before responding in heated discussions.
- Repeating the question or statement internally to process it more fully.
- Stepping away if necessary, allowing emotions to settle before continuing the conversation.

This simple pause gave Mark time to evaluate his emotions, check his assumptions, and choose a response that aligned with his values.

How to Apply This: Next time you feel triggered, practice pausing before speaking. If possible, take a short break before responding to give your mind a chance to engage rationally rather than emotionally.

2. Engage in Intellectual Exercises to Strengthen Cognitive Flexibility

Just as physical exercise strengthens the body, mental exercises enhance our ability to think clearly, consider alternative viewpoints, and navigate complex discussions with ease.

Mark found debating both sides of an argument incredibly helpful. By challenging his own perspective, he became more open to nuance and less defensive in discussions.

He also:

- Read books and articles from differing viewpoints to expand his understanding.
- Practiced summarizing opposing opinions before responding, ensuring he fully understood the other side.
- Asked himself, "What would I believe if I had grown up in a different culture?" to increase intellectual empathy.

How to Apply This: Choose one topic you feel strongly about. Challenge yourself to engage with opposing viewpoints, not to change your beliefs but to broaden your understanding.

3. The "Is It True?" Method: Challenging Emotional Distortions

One of the biggest breakthroughs for Mark was realizing that not all of his thoughts were accurate. He often assumed the worst—believing, for example, that if someone disagreed with him, they must dislike him.

By practicing the "Is It True?" method, he learned to question emotional assumptions before accepting them as reality.

Whenever strong emotions arose, he asked himself:

- Is this thought factually true, or am I making assumptions?
- What evidence supports or contradicts this belief?
- How might a calm, rational person interpret this situation?

By reframing his thoughts in this way, Mark was able to regain clarity and respond thoughtfully rather than emotionally.

How to Apply This: The next time you catch yourself in negative self-talk or emotional assumptions, ask: "Is this objectively true, or am I distorting reality?"

Biblical Insight: Emotional Stability as a Path to Wisdom

> "The wise in heart are called discerning, and gracious words promote instruction." (Proverbs 16:21)

This verse highlights the connection between wisdom, emotional regulation, and communication. Wise individuals do not react impulsively—they pause, reflect, and respond with discernment. Emotional stability fosters rational engagement, allowing us to engage with truth, grace, and clarity.

Your Next Steps Toward Emotional and Intellectual Clarity

Emotional regulation is not just about feeling better—it's about thinking better, engaging better, and building stronger relationships.

- This week, choose one strategy to implement:
- Pause before responding in emotionally charged situations.
- Engage in intellectual exercises—debate an opposing viewpoint, read from a different perspective, or summarize someone else's position before responding.
- Use the "Is It True?" method to challenge negative thoughts and emotional distortions.

Each of these small actions will help rewire your brain for clarity, wisdom, and healthier relationships. As you develop emotional regulation, your intellectual depth and relational stability will grow in ways you never imagined.

Which step will you take today to move toward deeper clarity and emotional wisdom?

The Journey Ahead: Lifelong Growth and Healing

Healing is not a one-time event or a final destination—it is an ongoing process of growth, self-awareness, and refinement. Just as a river carves its path over time, shaping the landscape with persistence and grace, so too does emotional healing transform us in ways that may not be immediately visible but are undeniably profound.

True healing is about more than simply overcoming struggles; it is about learning, evolving, and embracing the full depth of human experience—joy and sorrow, success and failure, certainty and doubt.

Chapter 12
Trust in Marriage

The Importance of Secure Attachment Within Marriage: Building a Foundation of Trust.

At the core of every thriving marriage lies a secure attachment—a deep, unshakable sense of trust and emotional safety between partners. When this foundation is strong, both individuals feel confident enough to be vulnerable, knowing that they will be met with understanding rather than rejection. But when emotional dysregulation disrupts this foundation, the relationship can become a battleground of fear, avoidance, or reactivity. Recognizing the impact of emotional dysregulation on attachment is the first step in strengthening the bond between partners and fostering a more secure, intimate connection.

How Emotional Dysregulation Affects Attachment

Attachment theory suggests that the way you connect with others in adulthood is deeply influenced by your early relational experiences. If you experienced consistent love, attunement—meaning a caregiver's ability to notice, understand, and respond to your emotional needs—and emotional responsiveness as a child, you likely developed a secure attachment style. This foundation allows you to form deep, trusting, and emotionally balanced relationships as an adult. However, if your early relationships were marked by inconsistency, emotional neglect, or relational trauma, you may have developed an insecure attachment style. This can show up in adulthood as difficulty trusting others, fear of abandonment, emotional dependency, or withdrawal.

Insecure attachment isn't a character flaw—it's a learned survival strategy formed in response to unmet emotional needs. Your nervous system adapted to protect you from further hurt, even if that means keeping people at a distance or clinging tightly out of fear.

The good news is that attachment styles are not fixed. With awareness, healing, and safe, consistent relationships—whether through friendships, partnerships, or therapeutic support—you can begin to repattern your attachment responses. You can learn to trust, connect, and experience emotional intimacy in ways that feel safe and fulfilling. Healing your attachment wounds is not just possible—it's transformative.

Consider the story of Lisa and Tom, a couple whose early years of marriage were marked by emotional misattunement—moments when one partner misses or misreads the other's emotional cues. Tom, having grown up in a household where emotions were suppressed, often reacted defensively during heated discussions. Lisa, on the other hand, had an anxious attachment style, craving reassurance but feeling abandoned when Tom withdrew. Their arguments followed a painful cycle—Lisa would pursue, demanding connection, while Tom would retreat, overwhelmed by the intensity of her emotions. This pattern deepened Lisa's insecurity and reinforced Tom's instinct to avoid confrontation.

It wasn't until they learned about attachment theory that they began to understand each other's emotional triggers. Rather than viewing their struggles as personal failures, they saw them as conditioned responses from past experiences. With this insight, they began practicing intentional connection—checking in with each other daily, sharing their emotions without fear of judgment, and reassuring one another during moments of distress. Over time, these small but significant changes rebuilt their foundation of trust, strengthening their emotional bond.

Strengthening Secure Attachment in Marriage

For couples seeking to build a secure and lasting bond, emotional awareness and consistency are essential. When you understand both your own and your partner's attachment styles, you're better equipped to navigate relational challenges with compassion instead of defensiveness. Rather than reacting out of fear or insecurity, you can respond with empathy, recognizing that many emotional responses are rooted in past relational patterns—not the present moment.

One of the most powerful ways to nurture attachment is by creating rituals of connection—small, consistent habits that reinforce emotional closeness. These daily or weekly practices don't need to be grand gestures. They can be as simple as:

- Expressing gratitude before bed
- Sharing a meal without distractions
- Taking a walk together
- Setting aside time for honest conversation

These small yet intentional acts send a steady, reassuring message: *I am here for you. I am safe. You can trust me.* Over time, they help both partners feel seen, valued, and emotionally secure.

Another critical pillar of secure attachment is vulnerability. If you've experienced emotional dysregulation or relational wounds, opening up may feel risky. You might fear being misunderstood, dismissed, or rejected. But true intimacy is built when both partners feel safe enough to share their fears, insecurities, and emotional needs. Vulnerability is an invitation: when you take the risk to be open, you create space for your partner to do the same. In that space, trust deepens.

Consistency in emotional support also reinforces secure attachment. It's not just about showing up during major life events—it's about being emotionally present in everyday moments. That might mean:

- Offering comfort after a stressful day
- Following through on your promises
- Being emotionally available during moments of distress

Each of these actions tells your partner's nervous system: This relationship is safe. I am not alone. I can depend on you.

By cultivating awareness, creating rituals of connection, practicing vulnerability, and showing up consistently, you and your partner can move toward a secure, emotionally connected relationship—one where both of you feel grounded, valued, and truly known.

When Professional Support Is Needed

For couples who find themselves stuck in destructive cycles—where emotional dysregulation leads to repeated conflict, avoidance, or deep-seated insecurity—seeking professional support can be invaluable. Therapy provides a neutral space for couples to explore their attachment patterns, develop healthier communication strategies, and break free from reactive relational habits. By working with a skilled therapist, partners can learn how to regulate their emotions together and build a foundation of lasting emotional security.

The Power of Gentle Communication in De-Escalating Conflict

Even in the healthiest marriages, conflict is inevitable. However, how couples handle disagreements determines whether these moments strengthen or weaken their connection. Reactivity—raising voices, defensiveness, or shutting down—can erode trust over time. In contrast, *gentle and intentional communication* preserves emotional safety, even in times of disagreement.

One practical strategy is the ***20-Minute Rule***—agreeing to take a break when emotions escalate, allowing both partners time to regulate their nervous systems before resuming the conversation. This prevents discussions from spiraling into attacks or shutdowns, creating a calmer environment for resolution.

Another valuable tool is using **"I" statements** to express emotions without assigning blame. Rather than saying, *"You never listen to me,"* which may provoke defensiveness, a partner could say, *"I feel unheard when I try to express my feelings."* This subtle shift fosters understanding rather than conflict.

Nonverbal communication also plays a crucial role in de-escalating tension. Soothing cues—lowering one's voice, maintaining open body language, or engaging in deep breathing—signal to the nervous system that the conversation is safe, reducing the likelihood of reactive responses.

Enhancing Emotional Security in Your Marriage

Take a moment to reflect on the ways emotional security manifests in your relationship. Do you and your partner feel safe expressing emotions without fear of judgment? Are there moments when one of you withdraws or becomes reactive due to past wounds? Consider discussing these insights together, focusing on one small shift that could enhance your emotional connection.

Biblical Wisdom: Love Rooted in Patience and Kindness

Throughout scripture, love is consistently described as patient, kind, and enduring. Proverbs 15:1 reminds us,

> *"A gentle answer turns away wrath, but a harsh word stirs up anger."*

This timeless wisdom speaks to the power of gentle communication in fostering emotional security. When couples prioritize kindness in their interactions, even during conflict, they create a relational environment that nurtures trust and stability.

1 Corinthians 13:4-7 provides a powerful blueprint for love:

> "Love is patient, love is kind. It does not envy, it does not boast, it is not proud. It does not dishonor others, it is not self-seeking, it is not easily angered, it keeps no record of wrongs. Love does not delight in evil but rejoices with the truth. It always protects, always trusts, always hopes, always perseveres."

Secure attachment mirrors this kind of love—it protects, trusts, and perseveres through challenges. By embracing patience and understanding, couples can fortify their bond, ensuring that their love remains a source of strength and security.

Applying These Lessons to Strengthen Your Marriage

Building a secure attachment takes intention, patience, and mutual effort. Consider choosing one of the following steps to apply in your relationship this week:

- Initiate a Ritual of Connection – Choose a simple daily or weekly practice that fosters closeness, such as expressing gratitude, sharing a meal without distractions, or engaging in a shared hobby.
- Practice Gentle Communication – The next time tension arises, try using an "I" statement instead of

blame, or introduce the 20-Minute Rule to create space for emotional regulation.

- Discuss Attachment Styles – Explore your attachment patterns together and identify how past experiences influence your interactions. Reflect on how you can create a safer emotional environment for each other.
- Seek Support if Needed – If unresolved patterns of emotional dysregulation persist, consider seeking professional guidance to deepen understanding and strengthen your connection.

Marriage is not about perfection but about *intentional growth.* By committing to emotional security, gentle communication, and consistent support, couples can cultivate a bond that is deeply rooted in trust, resilience, and enduring love.

Understanding the Cycle of Conflict in Marriage

Conflict is an inevitable part of any marriage, yet many couples find themselves trapped in repetitive arguments that never seem to reach a resolution. When emotional dysregulation is at play, even minor disagreements can spiral into painful confrontations. Recognizing the patterns within these conflicts allows couples to break free from destructive cycles and approach disagreements with greater emotional awareness and intentionality.

Imagine a couple who, despite their deep love for one another, struggle to navigate disagreements in a healthy way. Their arguments often follow the same painful trajectory—one partner feels unheard, reacts emotionally, and the other becomes defensive or withdraws. Without intervention, these unresolved conflicts can create emotional distance, making it harder to communicate effectively over time.

To begin understanding your own conflict patterns, consider reflecting on a few key questions: *What common themes tend to surface in our arguments? How do I typically react when tensions rise?* By exploring these questions, couples can uncover the underlying emotions that drive their conflicts and work together to approach disagreements more constructively.

How Emotional Flooding Disrupts Conflict Resolution

During an argument, emotions often run high, triggering a physiological response known as **emotional flooding**. When a person's heart rate exceeds 110 beats per minute, the brain enters survival mode, prioritizing emotional reactivity over logical reasoning. This explains why conversations that begin as minor disagreements can quickly escalate into full-blown arguments, leaving both partners feeling misunderstood and disconnected.

Consider Tina and Mark, a married couple who frequently argue over household responsibilities. Tina, feeling overwhelmed by the imbalance in chores, expresses frustration to Mark. But instead of engaging in the discussion, Mark withdraws, his body tensing as he shuts down emotionally. Frustrated by his silence, Tina raises her voice, desperate for a response. Mark, now feeling attacked, either leaves the room or responds with defensiveness. Their argument, originally about something as simple as dirty dishes, morphs into a painful cycle of blame, withdrawal, and emotional distance.

After seeking counseling, Tina and Mark learn a critical lesson: timing and regulation matter. By delaying discussions until both are emotionally grounded, they create space for more productive conversations. Rather than forcing dialogue in the heat of the moment, they establish a new rule: when tension rises, they take a break to calm their nervous systems before revisiting the issue. This simple adjustment transforms their ability to navigate disagreements with mutual respect.

Breaking the Cycle: Strategies for Conflict Resolution

Restoring healthy communication requires intentional strategies that address both emotional regulation and constructive dialogue. Couples who struggle with dysregulated conflict often benefit from structured techniques that guide them toward resolution.

One of the most effective approaches is the **"Repair Attempt"** strategy, which involves using a predetermined signal—such as a phrase or gesture—that communicates a need to pause before the argument escalates. This allows both partners to step away, regulate their emotions, and return to the conversation with greater clarity.

Another helpful practice is the **3-2-1 Method**, where each partner takes turns listing three things they appreciate about the other, two ways they could improve communication, and one goal for resolution. This exercise shifts the focus away from blame and toward strengthening the relationship.

Additionally, couples can implement a **Conflict-Resolution Routine**, setting aside a weekly check-in to discuss grievances in a structured, low-stress environment. By proactively addressing issues before they escalate, couples can prevent resentment from building and foster greater emotional intimacy.

To put these strategies into practice, reflect on a recent disagreement. *What emotions surfaced? How could a structured approach have helped de-escalate the situation?* Committing to even one small change—whether it's pausing before responding or shifting toward appreciation—can create a significant impact on the health of the relationship.

Biblical Wisdom for Navigating Conflict

Scripture offers timeless wisdom on handling disagreements with grace and patience. Ephesians 4:26 reminds us, *"Do not let the sun go down while you are still angry."* This passage emphasizes the importance of resolving conflicts in a timely manner, preventing resentment from taking root. While not every disagreement can be resolved in one conversation, making an effort to approach conflict with an open heart and a willingness to listen fosters emotional safety and mutual respect.

Similarly, Proverbs 15:1 states,

> *"A gentle answer turns away wrath, but a harsh word stirs up anger."*

When emotions are heightened, responding with gentleness rather than reactivity can completely shift the dynamic of an argument. A calm, measured approach invites understanding and connection, while impulsive words often fuel disconnection.

As you reflect on these biblical insights, consider how you can embody patience, kindness, and humility in your conflicts. Even in moments of frustration, choosing a tone of grace over accusation can transform not just individual disagreements but the overall emotional climate of your marriage.

Applying These Lessons in Your Relationship

Conflict resolution is not about eliminating disagreements altogether—it's about learning how to navigate them with wisdom and emotional regulation. To begin strengthening your approach to conflict, consider integrating one of the following practices into your relationship this week:

- Establish a "Time-Out" Plan – When tensions rise, agree to take a 20-minute break before continuing the conversation. This allows both partners to regain composure and prevents emotional flooding from taking control.
- Practice Gentle Communication – During your next disagreement, focus on using "I" statements rather than accusatory language. Instead of saying, "You never listen to me," try, "I feel unheard when we talk about this topic."
- Schedule a Weekly Check-In – Set aside time each week to discuss potential concerns in a low-stress

environment. Creating a space for open dialogue before conflicts escalate can significantly improve communication.
- Engage in a Gratitude Exercise – After a disagreement, take a moment to express appreciation for something your partner does well. Shifting focus toward gratitude fosters emotional connection even during difficult conversations.

Marriage is not about achieving conflict-free perfection, but about learning to engage in disagreements with mutual respect, patience, and emotional regulation. By practicing these strategies, couples can transform conflict from a source of disconnection into an opportunity for deeper understanding and intimacy.

Chapter 13
Loving the Dysregulated

Supporting a Loved One with Emotional Dysregulation

Supporting a loved one who struggles with emotional dysregulation can often feel like walking a tightrope. It requires striking the right balance—validating their emotions while holding them accountable, showing compassion without enabling, and offering care without falling into codependency. Without clear strategies, both individuals can become trapped in cycles that drain emotional energy and erode the foundation of their relationship.

Understanding how to provide support in a way that fosters growth rather than dependency is key. Whether you are navigating a romantic partnership, a friendship, or a family dynamic, learning to validate emotions without reinforcing unhealthy patterns, setting clear boundaries, and fostering effective communication will help you support your loved one without losing yourself in the process.

The Power of Validation in Emotional Regulation

Imagine a stormy sea, where waves crash violently against the shore, unpredictable and overwhelming. For someone struggling with emotional dysregulation, their inner world often feels just as chaotic. In these moments, validation becomes a lifeline, offering stability when emotions threaten to pull them under.

Validation does not mean agreeing with a person's perspective or endorsing their reaction. Rather, it is about acknowledging their emotions as real and understandable. When someone feels truly heard, their emotional intensity naturally decreases, allowing space for rational discussion. Conversely, when their feelings are dismissed or minimized, distress amplifies, often leading to further escalation.

Consider Emily, who frequently lashes out in anger when she feels ignored. Her husband, rather than reacting defensively or telling her to "calm down," tries a different approach: *"I see that you're really upset right now. Your feelings matter, and I want to understand what's wrong."* This simple statement helps Emily feel acknowledged, easing her emotional flooding and allowing for a more constructive conversation.

Why Validation Works

Validation has a profound neurological impact. Research shows that when individuals feel heard, the prefrontal cortex—the part of the brain responsible for logic and emotional regulation—activates, promoting rational thinking. Conversely, when emotions are dismissed, the amygdala, the brain's fear center, remains in overdrive, keeping the person stuck in distress.

This is why a well-placed validation statement can shift the direction of an emotional moment. Saying *"That sounds really difficult"* or *"I can see why you're feeling overwhelmed"* can help someone feel emotionally grounded, reducing their need to escalate the situation.

However, validation must be paired with reality. While acknowledging someone's emotions is crucial, reinforcing distorted thoughts can be harmful. Suppose a loved one frequently says, *"No one cares about me"* during moments of distress. Instead of agreeing or outright dismissing their statement, a balanced response might be: *"I know it feels that way right now, but is there evidence to support that? I care about you, and I know others do too."* This approach affirms their feelings without reinforcing unhealthy beliefs.

How to Validate Without Enabling

Providing validation without enabling requires careful communication. It is possible to acknowledge emotions while also setting boundaries and encouraging healthy coping strategies.

Take Mark and Sarah, for example. Mark struggles with emotional regulation and often spirals into self-pity when stressed, saying things like, *"Nothing ever works out for me. I might as well give up."* In the past, Sarah would try to solve his problems for him, reassuring him constantly and taking on the burden of fixing his distress. However, this approach left her emotionally drained and reinforced Mark's dependency on her.

Over time, Sarah learned a different approach. Instead of immediately stepping in to rescue Mark, she practiced validation paired with encouragement: *"I hear how hard this is for you, and I know it feels like things won't get better. But I also know you've handled tough situations before, and I believe in your ability to work through this."*

This response acknowledges Mark's emotions without reinforcing his sense of helplessness. It validates his feelings while gently encouraging resilience.

Practicing Validation in Everyday Conversations

Integrating validation into daily interactions can strengthen emotional connections and de-escalate tension. Some practical ways to implement validation include:

- Reflective Listening: Instead of immediately offering advice, reflect back what the other person is saying. "It sounds like you're feeling really frustrated because things didn't go the way you expected."
- Avoiding Judgmental Language: Refrain from phrases like "You're overreacting" or "It's not that bad." Instead, try "I can see why this would be upsetting."
- Balancing Validation with Reality: While affirming emotions, also gently challenge distorted thinking. If a loved one says, "Everyone is against me," respond with "I can tell you feel really isolated. Are there specific people who have made you feel that way?"

Biblical Insight: The Healing Power of Validation

The practice of validation aligns with biblical wisdom about compassion and understanding. Romans 12:15 encourages us to,

> *"Rejoice with those who rejoice; mourn with those who mourn."*

This verse highlights the importance of acknowledging another person's emotions, whether they are joyful or painful, without dismissing or minimizing their experience.

In supporting a loved one, our role is not to fix their feelings or invalidate them but to walk alongside them in understanding. This means listening, offering comfort, and gently guiding them toward a healthier mindset when necessary.

Applying Validation in Your Relationships

As you consider your own interactions, reflect on a recent conversation where a loved one was struggling emotionally. How did you respond? Did you offer validation, or did you find yourself minimizing their feelings or trying to "fix" the problem?

If you recognize areas where you can improve, consider how you might approach a similar conversation differently next time. Practicing validation is not about perfect responses but about fostering emotional safety and deeper connection in your relationships.

By learning to validate without enabling, you create a space where emotions can be acknowledged without being exaggerated, where support is given without fostering dependence, and where your loved one feels heard without losing the responsibility for their own healing.

Boundaries That Protect Both Partners

Healthy boundaries are the backbone of any stable relationship, particularly when emotional dysregulation is present. They serve as guidelines that protect both individuals from emotional harm while fostering mutual respect and understanding. Boundaries are not walls meant to shut others out, but rather structured pathways that allow for healthy connection without enmeshment or toxicity.

When emotional intensity runs high, communication can feel like navigating a minefield. One wrong word or perceived slight can ignite a storm of defensiveness, withdrawal, or hurtful exchanges. In these moments, it's essential to recognize when emotions are clouding rational thought and to implement strategies that preserve the integrity of the relationship.

The Challenge of Communication During Dysregulation

Emotional dysregulation can interfere with healthy communication, particularly during conflict. When one or both partners are emotionally overwhelmed, it becomes difficult to engage in constructive dialogue. The body's stress response takes over, shifting interactions from logical discussion to survival mode.

Imagine Jake and Rachel, a couple who often found themselves trapped in emotionally charged arguments. Jake, struggling with emotional dysregulation, would raise his voice and make impulsive, hurtful comments. Rachel, instead of reacting defensively or retaliating, recognized the signs of escalating tension. She calmly said, *"Let's take a break and talk when we're both calmer."* That simple decision to pause the conversation prevented an argument from spiraling into deeper resentment. Later, when emotions had settled, they revisited the discussion with clearer minds and a shared commitment to resolution.

Why Emotional Dysregulation Complicates Communication

During moments of emotional intensity, the brain's ability to process information logically diminishes. The prefrontal cortex, responsible for problem-solving and impulse control, takes a backseat while the amygdala—the brain's emotional alarm system—activates survival responses. These can manifest in different ways:

- Fight: The individual lashes out, using aggression or criticism to defend themselves.
- Flight: They disengage from the conversation, avoiding confrontation or withdrawing emotionally.
- Freeze: They become overwhelmed and unable to respond, often going silent or shutting down.
- Fawn: They immediately placate the other person, sacrificing their own needs to keep the peace.

Recognizing these reactions in yourself or your partner is the first step in de-escalating conflict before it causes lasting harm.

How to Establish Healthy Boundaries in Conflict

To navigate these highly reactive moments, couples can develop intentional communication strategies that protect both partners.

One of the most effective techniques is **pausing before responding**. Instead of reacting impulsively in the heat of an argument, take a deep breath, count to three, and give yourself a moment to think before speaking. This short pause can prevent regrettable words and create space for clarity.

Using **non-confrontational language** also reduces defensiveness. Rather than making accusations like, *"You always ignore me,"* reframe the concern with an "I" statement: *"I feel unheard when my concerns aren't acknowledged."* This shift in phrasing encourages open dialogue instead of triggering defensiveness.

Some couples find it helpful to establish a **safe word**—a neutral word or phrase either partner can use to signal the need for a pause in the conversation. This prevents escalation by allowing both individuals to take a step back without feeling like they are walking away from the issue altogether.

Additionally, practicing **active listening** can be a game changer. When one partner speaks, the other reflects back what they hear before responding. This ensures that emotions are acknowledged and reduces misunderstandings. Simple phrases like *"What I hear you saying is…"* or *"It sounds like you're feeling…"* can validate emotions while promoting clarity.

Lastly, it's essential to **revisit discussions later**, once both partners feel more regulated. If a conversation begins to escalate beyond control, agreeing to table it until emotions settle allows for resolution rather than further conflict.

Strengthening Your Communication Skills

Think back to a recent disagreement with your partner. Were there moments where emotions overpowered logic? How might using a pause, safe word, or reflective listening have changed the outcome? Consider implementing one of these techniques the next time tension arises and observe how it shifts the dynamic.

Navigating Conflict with Grace

Conflict is an inevitable part of any relationship. However, the way conflicts are handled can either deepen connection or create emotional wounds that linger long after the argument has ended. When emotional dysregulation is involved, conflicts often escalate quickly, leading to cycles of miscommunication, defensiveness, and resentment.

Mia and Sam's relationship was no exception. Arguments between them frequently left both feeling unheard and emotionally drained. One evening, after a particularly heated disagreement, they decided to take a different approach. Instead of reacting impulsively, they set aside time to calmly discuss their perspectives. They each expressed their feelings using "I" statements rather than blaming each other. What started as a recurring argument transformed into a conversation that strengthened their bond.

Keys to Conflict Resolution

One of the most effective ways to de-escalate conflict is by identifying the *underlying needs* driving the argument. Many disagreements are not actually about the surface-level issue but rather about unmet emotional needs—such as feeling unappreciated, unheard, or disconnected. Taking the time to ask, *"What am I really upset about?"* can bring clarity to the situation.

Establishing **ground rules for conflict** is another valuable strategy. Agreeing on principles such as no name-calling, no interrupting, and taking breaks when needed creates a sense of safety in discussions. This ensures that even difficult conversations remain respectful.

Additionally, shifting the mindset from "me versus you" to "us versus the problem" fosters a sense of teamwork rather than adversarial conflict. Instead of focusing on who is right, couples can ask, *"How can we solve this together?"* This reframe promotes collaboration and mutual understanding.

Taking responsibility for one's actions also plays a crucial role in conflict resolution. A simple but powerful phrase such as *"I realize I overreacted earlier, and I'm sorry"* can defuse tension and invite the other person to do the same. Acknowledging personal missteps creates an atmosphere where both partners feel safe admitting mistakes without fear of blame.

Finally, *celebrating progress* is essential. After successfully navigating a disagreement with improved communication, take a moment to acknowledge the growth. This reinforces positive patterns and strengthens emotional resilience for future conflicts.

Applying Conflict Resolution in Your Relationship

Consider a recent disagreement you had with your partner. What was the core issue? Were there unmet emotional needs that fueled the argument? What strategies could you have used to approach it differently? Reflect on one technique from this chapter that you can apply in your next challenging conversation.

Building Emotional Resilience Together

Healthy relationships are not built on the absence of conflict, but on the ability to navigate disagreements with mutual respect and understanding. By setting boundaries, regulating emotions, and prioritizing constructive communication, couples can create a foundation of trust that withstands life's inevitable challenges.

As you implement these strategies, remember that progress takes time. Each effort to pause before reacting, listen with empathy, and communicate with intention strengthens not only your relationship but also your own emotional resilience.

If you and your partner struggle with recurring conflicts, commit to one small shift this week—whether it's using a safe word, practicing reflective listening, or identifying underlying needs during disagreements. Small changes can lead to profound transformation over time.

> "Do not let the sun go down while you are still angry." (Ephesians 4:26)

This biblical wisdom reminds us that unresolved anger can fester, making conflict resolution a crucial part of emotional and relational healing. By addressing challenges with patience, grace, and understanding, we foster relationships that are not only enduring but deeply fulfilling.

Chapter 14
Trust in Parenting

Secure Attachment in Parenting and Marriage: Healing Generations Through Emotional Safety

At its core, secure attachment provides a profound sense of emotional safety—a stability that transforms both marriage and parenting. When you're securely attached, you are able to be present in your relationships with emotional availability, empathy, and resilience. Disagreements with a spouse or emotional outbursts from a child no longer feel like personal threats. Instead, they become opportunities for connection, growth, and understanding.

Just as secure attachment forms the foundation for emotional stability in marriage, it is equally essential in parenting. For parents, this means being consistent and responsive, without placing the burden of their own unmet emotional needs on their children. Securely attached parents don't rely on their children—or their spouse—to regulate their emotions. Instead, they model emotional regulation, empathy, and healthy boundaries, allowing relationships to thrive even in the face of difficulty.

However, when emotional dysregulation or unresolved attachment wounds are present, insecure attachment styles—such as anxious, avoidant, or disorganized—can shape our reactions in both marriage and parenting. A spouse needing space may feel like abandonment. A child's frustration may be misinterpreted as disrespect. These interpretations don't reflect the current moment—they echo old wounds crying out for healing.

By cultivating secure attachment within yourself and your marriage, you lay a solid emotional foundation that extends naturally to your children. This foundation creates a home environment where trust, connection, and emotional safety are the norm. Children raised in this environment learn that their feelings are valid, their voices are heard, and their relationships are safe.

Healing generational patterns begins with our own transformation. When we move from wounded to whole, we stop reacting out of fear and start responding out of love—shaping the emotional legacy we pass on to the next generation.

A Marriage Transformed by Attachment Awareness

Consider Susan, who struggles with *anxious attachment*. When her husband, Ryan, spends time alone or becomes quiet, she panics, fearing it means he no longer loves her. Her emotions escalate. She seeks constant reassurance, asks repeated questions, and sometimes lashes out. Over time, Ryan feels overwhelmed, and rather than drawing closer, he begins to pull away—unintentionally confirming her worst fears.

But something begins to shift when they both recognize the attachment dynamic at play. Together, they create rituals of reassurance—a nightly check-in where Ryan intentionally expresses his love and emotional availability. This small but consistent act becomes a lifeline, calming Susan's nervous system and strengthening their bond.

Extending Security to Children: The Ripple Effect of Healing

The same principles apply in parenting. When a child experiences consistent emotional attunement, they internalize a powerful message: *my emotions are safe here*.

A securely attached parent doesn't punish a child for feeling big emotions—they welcome them, guiding the child through them with empathy and calm. This helps the child develop self-regulation skills, knowing they are safe, valued, and loved regardless of their emotional state.

When your child is met with warmth instead of shame, curiosity instead of control, validation instead of dismissal, their internal world begins to feel safe. Over time, they learn to regulate their own emotions—not out of fear of upsetting you, but because they've experienced what it's like to be emotionally understood and supported.

Breaking the Cycle, One Secure Connection at a Time

Healing your own attachment wounds is not just for your benefit—it's a legacy you pass on. When you and your partner practice secure attachment, you create a relational environment where your children can thrive, emotionally and developmentally.

This journey doesn't demand perfection. It invites awareness, consistency, and compassion. As you become a safe place for your partner, you become a safe place for your child. And in doing so, you break generational cycles and replace them with emotional stability, healthy connection, and lasting love.

Strengthening Secure Attachment in Relationships

Developing secure attachment requires intentional effort in both marriage and parenting. One of the most powerful ways to foster security is by creating *rituals of connection*—daily moments that reinforce emotional closeness. In a marriage, this could be sharing a quiet cup of coffee in the morning, exchanging words of affirmation before bed, or practicing active listening during stressful moments. For parents, it could be a bedtime routine that includes storytelling, checking in about their day, or offering a comforting hug after a tough moment. These small but meaningful gestures build *emotional safety*, reassuring partners and children that they are valued and understood.

Another key component of secure attachment is the *repair process*—the ability to acknowledge mistakes, apologize, and reconnect after conflict. No relationship is perfect, and moments of emotional mis-attunement are inevitable. However, it is the act of repairing these ruptures that strengthens the bond.

Imagine Sarah, a mother who has had a long, exhausting day. When her teenage daughter rolls her eyes in frustration, Sarah snaps, reacting more harshly than she intended. Later, recognizing her overreaction, she sits down with her daughter and says, "I was stressed and overreacted earlier. I'm sorry for snapping at you. That wasn't fair." Her daughter, initially defensive, softens—because the simple act of parental humility and accountability reaffirms their bond.

Children learn emotional regulation by witnessing their parents model it. When parents own their mistakes and repair emotional ruptures, they teach children that conflict is not something to fear but something to navigate with honesty and grace.

Creating a Secure Base for Your Children

As your children grow into emerging adults, they're not just learning to navigate the world—they're building an internal blueprint for how to connect, trust, and regulate their emotions. This blueprint, known as an attachment framework, will shape how they approach relationships, process their emotions, and form their identity. And they need you—*not a perfect parent*, but a present, emotionally stable one—to serve as their secure base.

When you're emotionally available and consistent, you provide the stability, safety, and guidance they need to thrive. But if you're carrying the weight of arrested development or unresolved trauma, it's easy to unknowingly pass that weight onto your child. Instead of receiving support, they may feel the subtle pressure to meet your emotional needs—becoming a caretaker when they should be the one being cared for.

This role reversal is more than unfair—it's damaging. It teaches children that love must be earned, that their needs are secondary, and that emotional safety is unpredictable. And unless these patterns are addressed, the dysfunction gets handed down, generation after generation.

But here's the hope: you can interrupt that cycle.

When you begin doing your own inner work—healing attachment wounds, learning emotional regulation, and growing in relational maturity—you become the stable foundation your child needs. You model what it means to be emotionally healthy. And you create a home where love is safe, consistent, and secure.

Emotional Stability: The Foundation of Healthy Parenting

Emotional stability in parenting is like the sturdy frame of a house—everything else is built upon it. That stability doesn't come from being perfect. It's built through awareness, intentionality, modeling, and repair. Every interaction with your child becomes an opportunity—not just to teach, but to grow together.

One of the most powerful tools you have as a parent is emotional validation. When your child is upset, your instinct may be to minimize or fix the problem: "It's not a big deal," or "You're fine." But healing and security come when you slow down and make space for their feelings:

"I see that you're really frustrated right now. I'm here with you. Let's work through this together."

This simple shift not only soothes your child—it teaches them how to understand and manage their emotions, laying the foundation for lifelong emotional intelligence and self-regulation.

Secure attachment also requires boundaries wrapped in compassion. Being a safe parent doesn't mean saying yes to everything—it means providing structure that is consistent, respectful, and loving. Children thrive when they know what to expect and trust that you'll show up with both strength and kindness.

Take Mark, for example. He struggles to set limits with his five-year-old son, Daniel. In the past, Mark gave in to tantrums, trying to avoid conflict—but in doing so, he reinforced the behavior. Once Mark learned to stay calm, validate Daniel's feelings, and hold firm boundaries, things began to shift.

"I know you're upset. It's okay to feel mad, but it's not okay to throw things. I'll be here when you're ready to talk."

This approach helped Daniel learn that emotions are safe—but so are boundaries. Over time, he felt more secure, because his dad became someone he could trust, even in the middle of big feelings.

The Power of Apology in Attachment Repair

No parent gets it right all the time. And that's okay. Secure attachment isn't built through perfection—it's built through repair.

Humility is one of the most powerful tools you have. When you miss the mark—whether it's snapping at your child, emotionally withdrawing from your spouse, or dismissing someone's feelings—an honest apology can transform a moment of disconnection into one of reconnection.

In marriage, this might sound like:

"I realize I shut down during our argument. I know that made you feel unheard. I want to work on that."

In parenting, it could be:

"I didn't listen closely earlier, and I'm sorry. What you're feeling matters to me."

These simple but sincere moments create ripples of trust that shape your family's emotional culture. Your children don't need you to be flawless—they need to see that love can withstand mistakes, and that relationships can be mended, not broken, when conflict arises.

Breaking the Cycle and Building a Legacy of Safety

When you do the inner work of becoming a securely attached partner and parent, you're not just creating a healthier present—you're shaping a different future. You're breaking the cycle of emotional instability and modeling a way of being that says: *love is safe, feelings are welcome, and connection is always possible.*

Your healing becomes your child's foundation. And from that secure base, they'll grow with confidence, resilience, and the freedom to become who they were created to be.

Biblical Insight: Restoring Trust in Relationships

Reflecting on the wisdom of **Ephesians 4:32**,

> *"Be kind to one another, tenderhearted, forgiving one another, as God in Christ forgave you,"*

We see that emotional healing is deeply intertwined with forgiveness and grace. A secure relationship—whether with a spouse or a child—is built on compassionate understanding rather than perfection. By extending grace to ourselves and others, we foster an atmosphere where love is not conditional on performance, but steadfast and enduring.

Applying These Lessons: Steps Toward Emotional Security

To cultivate a more secure, loving relationship—whether in marriage or parenting—consider these actionable steps:

- Identify One Personal Emotional Trigger – Recognizing what activates insecurity or reactivity allows you to respond rather than react.
- Create Daily Reassurance Rituals – Whether it's checking in with a spouse at night or setting aside intentional time with a child, small moments of connection reinforce emotional safety.
- Practice Repairing Relational Ruptures – Make it a habit to acknowledge mistakes and apologize, reinforcing the security of the relationship.
- Model Emotional Regulation – Instead of reacting impulsively, demonstrate self-regulation strategies, such as pausing before responding or using grounding techniques.

- Reframe Conflict as an Opportunity for Growth – Instead of seeing disagreements as threats, view them as chances to deepen understanding and build resilience.

Secure attachment is a journey, not a destination. Each effort to build trust, consistency, and emotional safety—whether in a marriage or with a child—creates stronger, more resilient relationships. By embracing awareness, repair, and grace, we break free from patterns of emotional dysregulation and create a foundation of lasting love and stability.

Chapter 15
An Emotionally Regulated Family

Building a Family Culture of Emotional Regulation

Creating a home where emotional regulation is modeled, practiced, and valued begins with intentionality. As a parent, you set the emotional tone of your home—shaping not only how emotions are expressed and managed, but also how they are understood.

Imagine a family dinner where each person shares one high and one low from their day. This simple ritual may seem small, but it fosters emotional awareness, communication, and connection. When children see their parents openly and constructively discussing their emotions, they begin to internalize the message: *feelings are welcome here.*

Encouraging your children to express emotions without fear of judgment is essential. Let them know it's okay to feel angry, sad, excited, or overwhelmed. What matters most is how they process and express those emotions, and what they choose to do when those feelings lead to action.

But more powerful than anything you say is what you *show*. Your children learn emotional regulation by watching you. When they see you handle stress with grace, pause before reacting, and speak with empathy—even in frustration—they begin to mirror those same behaviors.

Likewise, when they witness you respecting boundaries, upholding values, and treating others with dignity, it leaves an imprint. But if they see you lashing out, dismissing others, or disregarding emotional or relational boundaries, that pattern becomes part of their learning as well.

The Truth is: You Are Their Blueprint.

As you move forward in building a family culture of emotional health, consider weaving in *intentional practices* that create safety, routine, and relational warmth:

- Daily check-ins or reflection rituals
- Emotion-naming games for younger children
- Calming spaces or quiet breaks when emotions run high
- Regular conversations about empathy, accountability, and repair

These simple, consistent practices will help your children learn that emotions are not problems to fix—but invitations to connect, grow, and understand themselves more deeply. And through your example, they'll come to know that regulation is not about control—it's about relationship.

Modeling Emotional Awareness

One of the most effective ways to teach emotional regulation is to **practice it yourself**. Children and even teenagers absorb emotional habits by watching their parents. When you vocalize your emotions in a calm and reflective way, you show them that emotions are not something to fear or suppress. Instead of reacting impulsively to frustration, take a breath and say, *"I'm feeling a bit anxious today, so I need some quiet time to recharge."* These small moments of self-awareness teach children that emotions are normal and manageable.

Beyond verbal modeling, be mindful of **nonverbal cues**. A child may not always understand what you're saying, but they are always observing how you respond to stress. If your body language and tone remain composed during conflicts, they will learn to mirror that regulation.

Teaching Coping Strategies as a Family

Rather than teaching coping mechanisms as a reaction to emotional outbursts, incorporate them into everyday life. Engaging in stress-reducing activities as a family—like deep breathing, stretching, or taking short walks—normalizes self-soothing techniques.

Consider implementing **playful emotion regulation exercises**, such as turning deep breathing into a game. Have young children blow "bubbles" with slow, intentional breaths or pretend to be a balloon inflating and deflating. These fun activities make emotional regulation feel less like a chore and more like a natural part of family life.

Older children and teens benefit from journaling, art, or movement-based coping strategies. Encourage them to write down their feelings after a tough day, go for a mindful walk, or listen to music that helps them process emotions. By making these strategies part of everyday routines, they become second nature.

Celebrating Emotional Growth

Acknowledging and reinforcing emotional progress is just as crucial as teaching regulation skills. When your child successfully manages a difficult situation—whether it's calming themselves after frustration or expressing their needs without a meltdown—celebrate their effort. This doesn't mean rewarding every small achievement but rather recognizing growth through affirmations: *"I saw how you took a deep breath before responding to your sister. That was really mature."*

This type of reinforcement strengthens the child's motivation to regulate emotions, helping them feel proud of their ability to handle challenges. Over time, they will develop **self-awareness and resilience**, equipped with the confidence to navigate emotions independently.

Fostering Emotional Intelligence in the Home

Emotional intelligence (EI) is the ability to recognize, understand, and manage one's own emotions while also being sensitive to the emotions of others. In a home where EI is nurtured, relationships flourish, conflict is reduced, and emotional resilience is strengthened.

Children primarily learn emotional intelligence by observing their caregivers. When parents model empathy, patience, and emotional regulation, children internalize those behaviors and begin to mirror them. Research shows that high EI enhances a person's ability to manage stress, navigate conflict, and build meaningful relationships.

Take Karen, a mother of three, who noticed her eldest child struggling with frustration. Instead of simply instructing him to calm down, she modeled emotional awareness by saying, "I'm really tired right now, so I need a few minutes to sit quietly before we talk." Her children began to adopt this approach, learning to name their feelings and pause before reacting.

Similarly, Sarah, also a mother of three, once felt overwhelmed by her children's emotional outbursts. But as she began to understand EI, she recognized patterns in their behavior—triggers like hunger, fatigue, or school stress. By validating their feelings and helping them identify emotions, she fostered a calmer, more respectful household.

Emotional intelligence is not an inborn trait but a learnable skill. When families commit to recognizing emotions, expressing them constructively, and practicing self-regulation, they build a home environment grounded in empathy, understanding, and emotional stability.

Practical Strategies for Cultivating Emotional Intelligence

Building emotional intelligence as a family requires intentionality, practice, and open conversations. In many homes, emotions go unspoken, leading to misunderstandings, bottled-up frustrations, or reactive behaviors like anger and avoidance. Creating a culture where emotions are acknowledged and discussed helps family members develop self-awareness, empathy, and emotional regulation.

Begin by reflecting on how emotions are currently expressed in your home. Do family members feel safe sharing how they feel, or are certain emotions dismissed or ignored? Recalling recent emotional moments can reveal patterns and offer opportunities for healthier responses.

A practical way to nurture emotional intelligence is by introducing a family emotions chart. This visual tool helps children expand their emotional vocabulary, moving from vague expressions like "I'm mad" to more precise ones such as "I feel disappointed because I was left out at recess." Clearer emotional language leads to more effective communication and problem-solving.

Another helpful strategy is the Feel-Think-Do Exercise, which encourages thoughtful responses rather than impulsive reactions. When emotions run high, guide family members to pause and ask:

- What am I feeling?
- What am I thinking about this situation?
- What should I do next?

This simple framework fosters emotional awareness and self-regulation. When practiced consistently, it equips children and adults alike with lifelong tools for managing emotions, resolving conflict, and strengthening relationships.

Establishing Routines That Promote Stability

In the whirlwind of daily life, routines act as an anchor, offering stability, emotional regulation, and stronger family connections. Predictability provides a sense of safety and control—especially for children—helping reduce anxiety, improve behavior, and foster emotional resilience.

The brain naturally craves structure. When children know what to expect, they feel more secure and are better able to manage their emotions. Simple, consistent routines—such as shared meals, bedtime rituals, and emotional check-ins—can transform a chaotic household into one that nurtures calm, connection, and cooperation.

Consider the Johnson family. Their mornings used to be filled with stress—rushed breakfasts, forgotten items, and tense departures. But after introducing a morning ritual that included a shared breakfast, a quick check-in, and packing bags the night before, the atmosphere changed dramatically. The shift from chaos to consistency brought emotional ease and stronger relational bonds.

Or take John and Melissa, who were frequently overwhelmed by rushed mornings. They implemented a simple routine: a quiet breakfast, a five-minute family check-in, and a predictable departure time. Within weeks, emotional outbursts and stress diminished, and the family began their days with calm and connection.

How Routines Support Emotional Regulation

Predictability reduces stress: When expectations are clear, children feel more in control and less anxious.

Structure teaches self-discipline: Consistent routines promote responsibility and emotional self-regulation.

Rituals foster connection: Shared daily practices—like family meals or bedtime stories—build trust, safety, and emotional security.

Practical Strategies for Building a Supportive Family Structure

- Create Consistent Daily Routines. Set regular times for meals, bedtime, and emotional check-ins. These simple anchors provide stability.
- Use Emotion Time-Outs. Encourage family members to take space to self-regulate during emotionally charged moments before returning to resolve conflict.
- Celebrate Stability. Acknowledge when routines are followed or emotions are managed well. This reinforces positive habits and creates a sense of progress.
- Incorporate Connection Moments. Use mealtimes, morning greetings, or bedtime reflections as emotional touchpoints where family members can share feelings and experiences.

Takeaway Action: Start with One Routine This week, introduce one new consistent practice—whether it's a structured morning, an intentional bedtime routine, or a regular family meal. Observe how this simple shift impacts the emotional climate of your home. Small, consistent changes can lay a strong foundation for lasting emotional health and connection.

Applying These Lessons: Creating a Culture of Emotional Awareness

To integrate emotional regulation into family life, consider these actionable steps:

- Model emotional awareness daily by verbalizing and managing your emotions in front of your children.

- Introduce simple family rituals that promote emotional connection, such as sharing highs and lows at dinner.
- Practice structured emotional intelligence exercises, like using an emotions chart or the "Feel-Think-Do" reflection.
- Reinforce stability through routines that provide comfort and consistency, reducing anxiety and emotional distress.

By embedding these habits into daily life, you foster emotional intelligence, resilience, and deeper familial connections. Your home becomes a sanctuary of understanding, love, and regulation—a place where emotions are not feared but embraced, understood, and managed with grace.

How Family Meetings Foster Emotional Regulation and Connection

Regular family meetings serve as an emotional anchor in the home, creating a structured space for open communication, conflict resolution, and meaningful connection. These gatherings give each family member a voice—offering a safe environment to express joys, concerns, and needs—while reinforcing the family's shared values and goals.

In a world where daily stress often leads to miscommunication and emotional bottlenecks, intentional check-ins provide a pressure release valve. Rather than letting frustrations accumulate and explode, families can process emotions together in a calm, predictable setting that promotes understanding and unity.

Why Family Meetings Matter for Emotional Health

The benefits of family meetings go far beyond managing schedules or assigning chores. From a psychological standpoint, they support emotional regulation and relational health in key ways:

- Reducing Miscommunication. Many family conflicts stem from assumptions and misunderstandings. Regular meetings clarify expectations and ensure everyone feels heard before issues escalate.
- Preventing Emotional Bottlenecks. When emotions are ignored, they accumulate and eventually erupt. Family meetings offer a constructive outlet for emotional expression, reducing the risk of outbursts or resentment.
- Providing Predictability and Safety. Consistent meetings create a rhythm of communication that builds emotional security. Knowing there is a reliable space to speak openly helps children and adults develop trust and self-awareness.

Take the Martinez family, for example. Every Sunday night, they hold a 30-minute meeting where each person shares a high and a low from their week. Over time, this simple routine has created a culture of emotional openness and reflection. Their children have learned that talking about feelings is not only allowed—it's encouraged.

Similarly, the Ramirez family once struggled with ongoing conflict and missed connections. After implementing weekly meetings to discuss both logistical and emotional matters, they noticed a dramatic shift. Tension decreased, trust grew, and their relationships deepened through consistent, intentional communication.

Therapeutic Strategies for Effective Family Meetings

- Schedule Regularly. Choose a consistent day and time each week that works for everyone. Treat this time as sacred—just as important as any work, school, or church commitment. Even 15 minutes can make a difference when practiced regularly.
- Create a Safe, Respectful Space. Foster emotional safety by establishing ground rules. Use a "talking object" to ensure only one person speaks at a time.
- Avoid blame or criticism; instead, use "I" statements to express feelings.
- Focus on solutions rather than past mistakes.

Use a Simple Meeting Structure:

- Check-in. Each person shares a "high" and a "low" from their week.
- Discussion. Address any concerns, needs, or upcoming events.
- Reflection. Talk about one way the family can support each other in the coming week.
- End with Encouragement. Conclude meetings with gratitude or affirmations. A simple compliment or word of appreciation strengthens connection and reinforces positive interactions. For example, a child might say, "Dad, I liked how you helped me with my homework," while a parent might respond, "I'm proud of how you handled your frustration today."

Takeaway Action: Start Your Own Family Meeting This Week

Choose a time, set a simple agenda, and invite each family member to share. Start small and focus on creating a consistent, respectful space. Over time, you'll likely find that these moments of connection transform how your family communicates, solves problems, and supports one another emotionally.

Biblical Insight: The Power of Gathering Together

The Bible repeatedly emphasizes the importance of regular connection and encouragement within a community—whether within families, friendships, or faith groups.

> "Let us not give up meeting together... but encourage one another." (Hebrews 10:25)

This verse highlights that consistent togetherness fosters emotional and spiritual support. Just as fellowship in faith strengthens one's spiritual journey, regular family meetings nurture emotional and relational growth.

When families prioritize gathering with intentionality, they cultivate a foundation of love, understanding, and resilience.

Applying These Lessons: Creating a Culture of Connection

As you reflect on the power of family meetings, consider how you might integrate these strategies into your household.

- Choose a day and time for a weekly or biweekly family meeting.
- Create a safe structure by using a talking object and setting guidelines for respectful communication.
- End each meeting with affirmations or a moment of gratitude.

By fostering habits that prioritize emotional regulation, open communication, and connection, you're not only nurturing a harmonious family environment but also empowering each member to thrive emotionally. Over time, these small moments of intentional gathering will strengthen bonds, resolve conflicts before they escalate, and instill lifelong emotional intelligence in your children.

Start today—schedule your first family meeting, and watch how the simple act of gathering can transform the way your family connects.

Takeaway Action: Start a Daily Emotional Check-In

Make emotional conversations part of your family's routine. Start by sharing one emotional experience from your day at dinner. It could be as simple as, *"I felt really proud when I finished my work project today,"* or *"I felt frustrated when I got stuck in traffic."*

By modeling this practice, parents demonstrate emotional awareness, teaching children that it's okay to talk about feelings in a safe and supportive environment. Over time, this simple habit fosters greater empathy, patience, and connection within the family.

Bringing It All Together: Creating a Home That Fosters Emotional Growth

By developing emotional intelligence, establishing structured routines, and prioritizing family meetings, you lay the foundation for a home built on emotional awareness, connection, and stability.

This proactive approach breaks cycles of emotional dysfunction and nurtures lifelong resilience within your family. As emotions become easier to express, conflicts are resolved with greater patience and empathy, and relationships deepen.

Each of these steps cultivates an environment where emotions are understood, relationships are strengthened, and family members feel safe to grow. Embrace these changes and watch your home transform into a space of stability, trust, and lasting emotional connection.

Part 5
Long-Term Healing and Growth

Chapter 16 Shame and Self-Sabotage

Chapter 17 A Personal Healing Plan

Chapter 16
Shame and Self-Sabotage

Shame is one of the most powerful and destructive emotions tied to emotional dysregulation. It convinces individuals they are fundamentally flawed, reinforcing cycles of self-sabotage, isolation, and emotional instability. Unlike guilt, which acknowledges a mistake, shame attacks a person's identity, making healing feel impossible. For many, overcoming shame is the missing piece in their journey toward self-acceptance and emotional resilience.

To break free, we must first understand how shame fuels dysregulation, learn to challenge destructive self-talk, and embrace an identity rooted in grace and self-compassion.

How Shame Fuels Emotional Dysregulation

Shame is not just an uncomfortable emotion—it's a full-body experience. It activates the nervous system, triggering survival responses like fight, flight, freeze, or fawn. Imagine standing on a tightrope high above the ground—your body tenses, your breath shortens, and your mind races with fear. This is what shame feels like internally: a persistent state of insecurity, instability, and emotional exhaustion.

The Psychological Impact of Shame

Shame reinforces negative emotional patterns that keep individuals trapped in cycles of avoidance, self-sabotage, and emotional reactivity. Some respond by withdrawing completely, convinced they are unworthy of love or success. Others lash out, using anger to mask deeper feelings of self-loathing. Some engage in destructive coping mechanisms—overeating, substance abuse, self-isolation, or perfectionism—in an attempt to numb or overcompensate for their feelings of inadequacy.

Over time, shame prevents growth. The brain resists change when shame is present, making self-improvement feel futile. It's like swimming against a powerful current—exhausting and discouraging.

Michael's Story: The Shame Cycle in Action

Michael grew up in a household where emotional expression was met with ridicule. As a child, if he cried, he was told to "man up." If he showed vulnerability, he was called weak. Over time, he internalized shame, believing he was defective for feeling deeply. As an adult, he suppressed his emotions until they erupted in explosive outbursts, reinforcing his belief that something was wrong with him.

Michael's story illustrates how shame becomes a self-fulfilling prophecy—it convinces us we are broken, and then we act in ways that reinforce that belief. But it also highlights the possibility of breaking free by confronting the lies shame tells us.

Breaking Free from Shame-Based Thinking

Shame thrives in silence, secrecy, and self-criticism. To overcome it, we must bring it into the light—naming it, challenging it, and replacing it with truth.

Reframing Shame as a Signal for Growth

Instead of seeing shame as proof of failure, reframe it as an opportunity for exploration and healing. Ask yourself:

- What is this feeling trying to tell me?
- Am I holding onto unrealistic expectations of myself?
- Is this shame based on truth, or is it a lie I was taught to believe?

By examining shame with curiosity rather than judgment, you **disarm its power** and create space for healing.

Practicing Self-Compassion Instead of Self-Criticism

Many people believe they need self-discipline and harsh criticism to grow. In reality, shame-based motivation is unsustainable—it leads to burnout, avoidance, and emotional shutdown. True transformation comes from self-compassion.

Consider how you would speak to a close friend struggling with shame. Would you say, *"You're a failure. You'll never change,"* or would you offer words of encouragement and understanding? Speak to yourself the same way:

- Instead of, "I always mess things up," try, "I am learning, and growth takes time."
- Instead of, "I don't deserve good things," try, "I am worthy of love and healing."

Self-compassion doesn't mean excusing mistakes—it means acknowledging your struggles while choosing to grow from them.

Recognizing and Challenging Shame Triggers

Shame often originates from past experiences and internalized beliefs. Identifying these triggers can help break the cycle. Ask yourself:

- Are there specific people, situations, or memories that make me feel ashamed?
- What core beliefs do I hold about myself because of shame?
- Are these beliefs true, or are they based on past wounds?

By recognizing these triggers, you can actively challenge and replace them with truth.

Overcoming Self-Sabotage: Breaking the Cycle of Shame-Driven Behavior

When shame is left unchecked, it leads to self-sabotage—patterns of behavior that prevent success, happiness, and personal growth. Some people procrastinate, fearing they'll fail anyway. Others avoid deep relationships, afraid of rejection. Some set impossibly high standards and then punish themselves when they fall short.

To break the cycle, it's essential to:

1. Identify Self-Sabotaging Patterns

Pay attention to how you react when things go well. Do you suddenly feel undeserving of success? Do you create unnecessary conflict or abandon your goals out of fear? These behaviors are often rooted in shame—the belief that you are not worthy of good things.

2. Rewrite Your Internal Narrative

Shame convinces you that you are defective, but your identity is not defined by past mistakes or struggles. Begin replacing shame-based thoughts with affirming truths:

- "I am allowed to experience joy and success."
- "I do not have to be perfect to be worthy of love."
- "My past does not define my future."

3. Take Small, Consistent Steps Toward Growth

Overcoming shame and self-sabotage isn't about making **huge, dramatic changes overnight.** It's about taking small, intentional steps in the right direction.

- If you struggle with self-worth, practice speaking kindly to yourself.
- If you avoid emotional vulnerability, share something small with a trusted friend.
- If you fear failure, set a realistic goal and take one small step toward it.

Progress, not perfection, is the goal.

Embracing a New Identity Rooted in Grace

Shame tells you that you are **too broken, too flawed, and too unworthy** to change. But this is a lie. Your worth is **not defined by your past, your mistakes, or the opinions of others.** Healing comes when you embrace the truth of who you are: **loved, valuable, and capable of growth.**

Biblical Perspective on Overcoming Shame

Scripture reminds us that we are not meant to live under the weight of shame.

- "There is now no condemnation for those who are in Christ Jesus." (Romans 8:1)
- "You are fearfully and wonderfully made." (Psalm 139:14)
- "I have loved you with an everlasting love." (Jeremiah 31:3)

Faith teaches that grace—not shame—defines our identity. When we accept that we are fully known and still deeply loved, shame loses its grip.

Takeaway Action: Release Shame and Step Into Grace

This week, challenge yourself to **let go of one shame-based belief**. Write it down, examine its origins, and replace it with truth. If your belief is, *"I am unworthy of love,"* replace it with, *"I am deeply loved and worthy of connection."*

By committing to this practice, you take a powerful step toward freedom from shame and self-sabotage—choosing growth, self-compassion, and healing instead.

Choosing Growth Over Shame

Shame convinces us we are broken beyond repair, but the truth is, healing is always possible. Breaking free from shame and self-sabotage requires courage, self-compassion, and a willingness to rewrite the narratives we've been taught to believe.

By recognizing shame's lies, challenging self-sabotaging behaviors, and embracing an identity rooted in grace, you break the cycle and step into a life of emotional freedom and self-acceptance.

Your past does not define you—but the choices you make today will shape your future. Choose growth. Choose healing. Choose grace.

Breaking Free from Destructive Self-Talk

Words hold immense power in shaping our identity. The way we speak to ourselves influences our self-worth, emotional regulation, and overall well-being. Negative self-talk, often driven by shame and past wounds, can become an internal script that reinforces feelings of inadequacy, keeping us stuck in patterns of self-doubt and emotional distress. To overcome shame and cultivate emotional resilience, we must **rewrite the narrative**—challenging destructive inner dialogue and replacing it with truth, grace, and self-compassion.

How Negative Self-Talk Fuels Emotional Dysregulation

Imagine standing in front of a mirror and hearing a voice repeat: *You're not good enough. You always mess things up. You'll never change.* Over time, these words become ingrained in your identity, influencing your emotions, behaviors, and decisions. Negative self-talk doesn't just shape perception—it **rewires the brain**, strengthening neural pathways that reinforce self-doubt and fear.

The Science Behind Self-Talk and Emotional Regulation

Self-talk is not just a reflection of our thoughts—it actively shapes our brain's neural pathways. Repeating negative messages deepens unhealthy mental patterns, much like walking the same path through a forest repeatedly. Over time, the trail becomes well-worn, making it the easiest route for our brain to take.

On the other hand, when we intentionally replace negative self-talk with positive, truth-based affirmations, we begin creating new neural pathways, making healthier thinking patterns more accessible. This process, known as neuroplasticity, allows us to rewire our brains toward self-compassion, confidence, and emotional balance.

Cognitive Distortions: The Lies We Tell Ourselves

Shame-based self-talk is often rooted in cognitive distortions—irrational thought patterns that reinforce negativity and emotional dysregulation. These distortions warp our perception of reality, making challenges seem insurmountable and self-worth feel conditional. Some common distortions include:

- Overgeneralization: I always fail at everything.
- Catastrophizing: If I make one mistake, my entire future is ruined.
- Emotional Reasoning: I feel unworthy, so it must be true.
- Personalization: If something goes wrong, it must be my fault.

These thought patterns fuel self-sabotage, perfectionism, and avoidance, keeping us trapped in cycles of emotional distress. The first step toward breaking free is recognizing these distortions and replacing them with truth.

Lisa's Story: The Power of Changing Self-Talk

Lisa was trapped in a cycle of self-condemnation. Every time she made a mistake, she told herself, *I ruin everything*. This belief wasn't based on reality, but on childhood experiences where she was blamed for things beyond her control.

Through therapy, Lisa began to challenge this destructive narrative. Instead of saying, *I ruin everything*, she learned to say, *I am learning and growing*. Though it felt unnatural at first, with consistent practice, her self-perception began to shift. She realized that her mistakes did not define her and that she was capable of growth.

Lisa's journey demonstrates the transformative power of self-talk. The words we repeat—whether they are words of defeat or encouragement—shape our reality.

Challenging Negative Self-Talk and Rewriting the Narrative

Shame-based thinking doesn't disappear overnight, but through intentional practice, we can break free from destructive self-talk and replace it with truth-based, compassionate language.

1. Challenge the Thought: Is It Based on Truth or Fear?

Negative self-talk often stems from past wounds rather than objective reality. Ask yourself:

- Is this thought factually true, or is it based on past pain?
- Would I say this to someone I love?
- What is a more balanced and compassionate way to view this situation?

For example, if you think, I'm a failure because I made a mistake, challenge that belief by saying, One mistake does not define me. I am capable of learning and improving.

2. Use an Affirmation Journal to Reinforce Positive Truths

Words hold power, and writing them down reinforces their impact. Start an affirmation journal, where you write down:

- Negative beliefs you struggle with (e.g., I'll never be good enough).
- Truth-based affirmations to replace them (e.g., I am worthy as I am, and I am growing every day).
- Small daily victories that reinforce your worth and progress.

Over time, these written truths rewire your mindset, creating new mental pathways of self-compassion and confidence.

3. Speak Life Over Yourself: The Power of Verbal Affirmation

Consider how powerful it would be if, instead of reinforcing shame, you spoke life over yourself daily. Imagine starting each morning by declaring:

- I am learning and growing, not failing.
- I deserve love and grace, even when I struggle.
- My past does not define me—my choices today shape my future.

Speaking these affirmations aloud may feel awkward at first, but with practice, it reshapes your inner dialogue and fosters emotional resilience.

Biblical Perspective: Words Carry Life or Destruction

The Bible speaks extensively about the power of words—not just those spoken aloud, but the ones we tell ourselves.

> "The tongue has the power of life and death."
> *(Proverbs 18:21)*

This verse reminds us that our words either build us up or tear us down. If we constantly criticize ourselves, we reinforce shame and self-doubt. But when we speak words of truth, grace, and encouragement, we set ourselves on a path toward healing.

Likewise, Romans 12:2 says:

> "Be transformed by the renewing of your mind."

Renewal happens when we actively replace harmful thought patterns with truth. When we choose grace over shame and truth over self-condemnation, we align with the identity of someone who is growing, healing, and deeply loved.

Rewriting Your Internal Narrative

To begin breaking free from destructive self-talk, try this practical exercise:

- Write down three negative statements you often tell yourself.
- Challenge each statement by asking, "Is this objectively true?"
- Rewrite each statement into a truth-based affirmation.

For example:

- Negative Thought: I always fail.
- Challenge: Is that true? Have I ever succeeded at anything?
- Truth-Based Reframe: I have faced challenges before, and I have overcome them. I am resilient and capable.

Commit to reading these truth-based affirmations daily. Over time, you will notice a shift in how you see yourself and how you handle challenges.

Choosing Truth Over Shame

Breaking free from destructive self-talk is a daily practice of choosing truth over lies, grace over condemnation, and self-compassion over shame. The way you speak to yourself matters—it shapes your emotions, your decisions, and your sense of worth. By challenging negative thoughts, using affirmations, and speaking life over yourself, you take control of your inner dialogue and transform the way you experience the world. Remember: Your past does not define you. Your struggles do not determine your worth. Your self-talk can either imprison you—or set you free. Choose words that heal. Choose words that empower. Choose words that align with truth.

Embracing a New Identity Rooted in Grace

Healing from emotional dysregulation and shame requires more than behavioral change—it necessitates a transformation in identity. Many who struggle with shame-based thinking find themselves trapped in a narrative that tells them they are broken, unworthy, or incapable of change. However, shifting from shame to redemption is possible when we embrace a new identity rooted in grace, truth, and self-compassion.

Shifting from Shame to Redemption

Shame often convinces us that we are defined by our past mistakes, emotions, or failures. It whispers lies that keep us bound in patterns of self-sabotage and fear. However, true healing begins when we recognize that shame is not our identity—it is merely a learned response that can be unlearned.

Chapter 17
A Personal Healing Plan

Overcoming Shame Through Therapy and Support

Michael spent years battling anxiety and anger. His emotional outbursts damaged relationships, and deep down, he believed he was *broken beyond repair*. The shame kept him isolated, preventing him from seeking help. Finally, after years of struggling, Michael decided to see a therapist specializing in *Cognitive Behavioral Therapy* (CBT).

Through therapy, he identified the negative thought patterns fueling his emotional reactions. He learned to pause, reflect, and challenge the self-condemning beliefs that had controlled him for so long. Seeking additional support, Michael joined a group therapy program where others shared similar struggles. Hearing their stories made him feel less alone, and over time, he replaced shame with self-compassion and resilience.

Michael's transformation didn't happen overnight, but with consistent effort, he learned to see himself through a lens of grace rather than shame. His journey is a testament to the power of seeking help and embracing a new identity beyond past failures.

Seeking the Right Professional Support

Healing from emotional dysregulation and shame often requires the right professional guidance. Unfortunately, many individuals seeking help are met with counselors who lack the specific training necessary for trauma recovery.

Finding the Right Therapist

If you are looking for a professional to support your healing, it's crucial to find someone with specialized expertise in emotional dysregulation, trauma, and self-sabotage recovery. Here's what to consider:

- Avoid general practice counselors: Traditional Licensed Professional Counselors (LPCs), Licensed Marriage and Family Therapists (LMFTs), and even some psychologists (PsyDs) may lack the training required for deep trauma work. While well-intentioned, they may inadvertently reinforce the very patterns you are trying to break.
- Look for Certified Trauma Specialists: Few traditional counselors receive any in-depth training in trauma, grief, or emotional dysregulation. Seek certified traumatologists who have pursued extensive post-graduate training in these areas.
- Request a Consultation before selecting your counselor: A competent trauma-informed therapist should offer a precommitment consultation (often free of charge) to assess whether they are a good fit for your specific needs. Use this opportunity to gauge their understanding of your experiences and their ability to articulate your struggles clearly.

- Seek Practical, Evidence-Based Therapies: Look for professionals trained in Dialectical Behavior Therapy (DBT), Cognitive Processing Therapy (CPT), or Internal Family Systems (IFS)—all of which offer proven strategies for managing emotional dysregulation.

Exploring Support Groups and Alternative Therapies

In addition to therapy, consider integrating **peer support** and **faith-based healing approaches** into your recovery:

1. Join a Trauma Recovery Support Group: Whether online or in-person, these groups provide a safe space to share experiences and gain encouragement.
2. Explore Faith-Based Healing Programs: Many churches and spiritual communities offer faith-based recovery programs focused on emotional healing and resilience.
3. Engage in Community Healing Activities: Attending personal development workshops, journaling groups, or structured recovery programs can reinforce new emotional habits.

Biblical Insight: Healing Through Wise Counsel

> "Plans fail for lack of counsel, but with many advisers, they succeed." (Proverbs 15:22)

Healing is not meant to be done in isolation. Seeking wise, trained professionals and trusted support networks can provide the guidance, accountability, and encouragement necessary for transformation.

If you haven't already, research professional counselors, trauma therapists, or support groups that specialize in emotional regulation and healing. Make a commitment to reach out to at least one this week and take the first step in seeking structured support.

Integrating Community into Your Healing Journey

Healing is not a solo endeavor. Community provides the relational safety needed to rewire patterns of emotional dysregulation. Many who struggle with shame and self-sabotage withdraw from others, fearing rejection or judgment. However, true transformation happens in relationships.

The Power of Connection in Healing

Humans are inherently social creatures. Neuroscience shows that healthy relationships regulate our nervous systems, reducing emotional volatility and reinforcing self-worth.

Being part of a supportive community offers:

- A Sense of Belonging: Knowing you are not alone in your struggles helps reduce shame and self-isolation.
- Emotional Accountability: Supportive relationships encourage growth, honesty, and self-awareness.
- Shared Wisdom: Hearing others' experiences can provide new insights and coping strategies for your own healing.

The Importance of Community in the Healing Process

Healing is not a journey meant to be walked alone. While the inner work of emotional growth is deeply personal, true transformation happens in relationships. Community provides the relational safety needed to rewire patterns of emotional dysregulation, offering both accountability and encouragement. Yet, many who struggle with shame and self-sabotage withdraw from others, fearing rejection or judgment. This isolation reinforces emotional instability, creating a cycle that only deepens feelings of unworthiness.

However, healing does not require perfection—it requires connection. When we engage with others in supportive relationships, we begin to experience the profound impact of being truly seen, understood, and accepted.

Why Community Matters in Healing

Humans are inherently social creatures. Our nervous systems are wired for connection, and neuroscience shows that healthy relationships regulate emotional responses, reduce volatility, and reinforce self-worth. When we feel supported, our brains release oxytocin, a hormone that promotes feelings of safety and trust. This is why being part of a nurturing community can serve as one of the most powerful tools for emotional regulation and healing.

- A healing-focused community provides:
- A Sense of Belonging
- Knowing that others share similar struggles helps dismantle the shame that comes with emotional

dysregulation. It allows individuals to realize they are not broken or alone, but rather part of a broader human experience.

- Emotional Accountability
- Supportive relationships encourage self-awareness and growth. When surrounded by people who understand the healing process, individuals are more likely to stay committed to their journey and recognize emotional setbacks as part of progress, not failure.
- Shared Wisdom and Perspective

Engaging with others provides valuable insights and alternative perspectives, helping individuals gain new coping strategies and emotional tools. Sometimes, hearing someone else's journey can illuminate a path forward that may have otherwise remained unseen.

Lisa's Story: Finding Strength Through Community

Lisa spent years battling emotional isolation after experiencing a traumatic event. She convinced herself that no one would understand her pain, so she withdrew, cutting off meaningful connections. The more she isolated, the stronger her feelings of shame and self-doubt became.

Eventually, she took a small but life-changing step—she joined a local trauma support group. At first, she hesitated to share her story, fearing judgment. But as she listened to others openly discuss their struggles, she realized something profound: she wasn't alone.

Slowly, Lisa began to share her emotions more freely. She discovered that her pain did not make her unworthy of connection—if anything, it deepened her ability to relate to and encourage others. Over time, she not only found healing for herself but also became a source of support for others in the group.

Lisa's story highlights an essential truth: community is not just about receiving support—it's about offering it. Healing is strengthened when we engage in mutual encouragement, understanding, and grace.

How to Integrate Community Into Your Healing Process

If you've been struggling alone, now is the time to step into connection. While it may feel intimidating at first, engaging in supportive relationships can be one of the most transformative steps toward healing.

Consider these practical ways to build a healing-focused community:

- Attend Local Workshops or Classes
- Look for events centered on emotional well-being, personal growth, or faith-based healing. These environments naturally attract like-minded individuals who value emotional development, making it easier to form meaningful connections.
- Engage in Volunteer Work
- Helping others creates a sense of purpose and fosters gratitude. It also provides opportunities to meet people who share similar values, reinforcing a sense of belonging.
- Build an Intentional Support Network

- Identify trusted friends, mentors, or faith leaders who can walk alongside you. A support network does not need to be large—it just needs to be intentional and made up of people who genuinely care about your growth.
- Create Healing Rituals with Others

Healing doesn't have to be done alone. Consider integrating shared rituals into your life, such as:

- Praying with a friend
- Joining a small group
- Attending a weekly Bible study
- Engaging in mindfulness or journaling exercises together

These *consistent practices* create stability and reinforce emotional regulation by making connection a regular part of your healing journey.

Biblical Insight: Strength in Relationships

> "As iron sharpens iron, so one person sharpens another." (Proverbs 27:17)

This verse reminds us that growth happens in relationships. We are meant to strengthen, support, and encourage one another. Healthy, intentional connections shape us into stronger, wiser, and more resilient individuals. Even in moments of pain or uncertainty, **God uses community as a source of healing, wisdom, and emotional renewal.** Choosing to engage with others—even when it feels uncomfortable—can be an act of faith, trusting that transformation often happens in the presence of others.

Stepping Into a New Identity

Healing is not just about managing emotions—it's about becoming the person you were created to be. Shedding the weight of shame, releasing self-sabotage, and embracing a new identity rooted in grace is a journey that requires:

- Intentional self-reflection
- Seeking professional support
- Building a community of healing

Every small step—whether it's challenging a negative thought, attending a support group, or speaking truth over yourself—moves you closer to emotional freedom. This week, take one tangible step toward engaging with your community.

Consider:

- Reaching out to a friend or mentor to share your emotional journey.
- Attending a support group, faith-based gathering, or workshop focused on healing and emotional growth.
- Volunteering in an area you are passionate about, allowing yourself to give back while building new connections.

Healing *requires* connection. You don't have to navigate this journey alone. By intentionally seeking community, you invite support, encouragement, and the powerful realization that you are not alone in this process. Who in your life can you reach out to today?

As you continue this journey, trust that you are not only breaking free from shame but stepping into a future of emotional resilience, self-worth, and grace.

Part 6
Summing the Parts

Bringing It All Together

In writing this book, I found it necessary to identify a set of core structural themes—a kind of scaffold—to support the story I wanted to tell and the truth I hoped to reveal. At its heart, this book has been an invitation to see beneath the surface: to recognize that emotional reasoning and dysregulation are not matters of stubborn willfulness or flawed character, but often the unintended outcomes of experiences beyond a person's original control. These wounds—unseen but deeply felt—can disrupt one's ability to safely engage with the world and with others.

From there, we explored the many ways a person's emotional framework can become compromised, often shaped by past trauma, family dysfunction, or long-standing relational wounds. We looked honestly at how those patterns show up in relationships, and how they can be named, understood, and ultimately transformed. We considered what it means to love and walk alongside someone affected by emotional dysregulation, and what it takes to chart a path toward restoration—both personally and relationally.

This final chapter is designed to bring all of that together. Here, the scaffold becomes visible. My goal is to provide a clear overview of the framework that has been woven throughout these pages—a way to help you reflect on what you've learned, revisit key insights, and carry forward a deeper understanding as you continue your own journey of healing and growth.

Insight 1: The Inner Landscape of Emotional Dysregulation

One of the most important truths woven through this book is that emotional dysregulation isn't a flaw—it's a response. It's not about being "too emotional" or "overreacting," but about the body and brain responding to old, unresolved pain as if it's happening again in the present. The emotional chaos so many of us feel—those moments when our heart races, our thoughts spin, and our reactions explode—often traces back to times in our lives when connection felt uncertain or unsafe.

These reactions usually begin in childhood, when we first learn how to interpret safety, connection, and love. If those early bonds were marked by inconsistency, neglect, or loss, our nervous system adapted to survive. And those adaptations—like constantly needing reassurance, lashing out when someone pulls away, or withdrawing when overwhelmed—can show up years later in our closest adult relationships.

When we hear about Lisa, for example, we see how her need for constant connection stems from a deep fear that people won't stay. Her emotional intensity isn't about drama—it's about survival. Jake's anger, too, masks a grief he never had space to express. His story reminds us that control can often be a shield for unspoken loss. And Anna's experience shows how easily small disagreements can become emotional landmines when fear of abandonment lives just under the surface.

These stories are here not to diagnose, but to help you see yourself with compassion. You are not broken—you are responding to wounds that have not yet been healed. But healing is possible. The book introduces powerful tools—like grounding techniques, mindful separation, and understanding your window of tolerance—that allow you to step out of old cycles and reclaim your peace. You begin to recognize when you're triggered, and instead of spiraling, you learn to pause, to breathe, and to choose a different response.

This is where your power begins: not in fixing everything at once, but in noticing. In choosing to stay present instead of reacting. In realizing that emotional storms don't have to rule your life—they can become signals that guide you back to safety. This insight sets the tone for the healing journey ahead: gentle, honest, and rooted in the belief that you are capable of more than just surviving—you can learn to thrive.

Insight 2: Healing as a Lifelong, Nonlinear Journey

Healing is not a straight line. It doesn't happen all at once, and it certainly doesn't happen just because we want it to. It's a messy, sacred, and deeply personal journey that unfolds over time—sometimes slowly, sometimes with setbacks, but always with the potential for growth.

This book reminds you again and again that healing is not about arriving at a perfect emotional state where nothing ever goes wrong. It's about returning—again and again—to practices that help you stay grounded, connected, and honest with yourself. There will be days when old patterns resurface and moments when it feels like you've made no progress at all. But the truth is, every time you choose self-awareness over shame, or take a pause instead of exploding, you are healing. Every choice matters.

Sarah's story captures this beautifully. For a long time, she felt like she was failing because her emotional triggers kept showing up. But over time, she began to recognize her progress—not in the absence of emotion, but in how she responded to it. Journaling helped her make sense of her thoughts. Gratitude shifted her perspective. And slowly, the grip of shame began to loosen. David's story mirrors this in a different way. He wanted healing to be fast and final, but what he found was something far deeper: the strength to trust God's timing, to lean into the process, and to keep moving forward—even when progress felt slow.

These stories remind us that healing isn't about being "done"—it's about choosing again and again to grow. One of the most powerful tools introduced is the 90-second pause. It's a simple idea: when you're emotionally triggered, take 90 seconds before responding. That space gives your brain time to shift from reaction to reflection. It sounds small, but that practice can change everything—from how you handle conflict to how you speak to yourself in moments of stress.

You don't have to fix everything today. You just have to stay in the process. This is a journey of grace and courage. Some days will feel like breakthroughs. Others will feel like setbacks. But through it all, the goal is not perfection—it's presence. As long as you keep showing up, healing is happening.

Insight 3: Building Secure Attachment and Emotional Safety

At the center of every strong relationship is a sense of emotional safety—the quiet, steady knowledge that we are safe to be seen, heard, and held without fear of rejection. But for those shaped by unstable or painful past relationships, emotional safety can feel foreign, even frightening. We long for closeness, yet fear abandonment. We crave connection, yet instinctively guard our hearts. This paradox becomes one of the most common threads in the struggle for relational health.

The book shows us that secure attachment isn't built on emotional intensity—it's built on consistency, trust, and a calm presence. When we learn to regulate our emotions, we stop needing others to do it for us. We can bring our full selves into a relationship without demanding, clinging, or running away. In the story of Susan and Ryan, we see this process unfold as they move from anxious reactivity to steady reassurance. It's not easy, but their willingness to show up again and again—with honesty and humility—lays the foundation for trust to grow.

Sarah's journey as a parent adds another layer to this insight . Her moment of emotional rupture with her child, and her choice to repair rather than shame or withdraw, becomes a turning point—not only for her child's development, but for her own healing. In modeling emotional repair, she offers her child a sense of security she never received herself—and in doing so, she rewrites part of her own story.

What's so empowering here is the reminder that attachment patterns are not fixed. They can be reworked, healed, and re-rooted in something more secure. This healing happens through daily emotional check-ins, family rituals, open conversations, and moments of mindful presence. These practices create a home—whether in marriage or in parenting—where everyone can breathe easier, speak more freely, and feel more deeply connected.

Insight 4: Healing From Betrayal and Relational Wounds

Few experiences shake the human spirit like betrayal. When trust is broken—especially by someone close—our entire emotional system goes into crisis. Betrayal triggers grief, confusion, rage, and often, a deep questioning of one's worth. But this book doesn't just explore the pain of betrayal—it gently walks you through the long, courageous process of healing.

We see this especially in the stories of Melissa and Sarah, two women deeply affected by relational betrayal. Their initial reactions—emotional flooding, vigilance, and self-doubt—are deeply human. Yet what unfolds is not just recovery—it's reclamation. Melissa begins to rebuild her sense of identity, slowly setting new goals and envisioning a future not defined by what was done to her, but by who she is becoming. Sarah's experience with forgiveness is especially powerful. Not the kind of forgiveness that forces reconciliation or denies pain, but the kind that sets her free from the emotional grip of resentment. Writing an unsent letter and praying for the person who hurt her became less about them and more about reclaiming her own peace.

This part of the journey is messy. The book is honest about that. Healing from betrayal involves waves of doubt, anger, and grief. But what emerges—when we stay in the work—is a clearer self, stronger boundaries, and a renewed understanding of love built not on fear or control, but on respect and mutual trust.

Insight 5: Faith as a Source of Emotional Resilience

Woven gently throughout the book is the thread of faith—not as a religious obligation, but as a deep, sustaining resource for those navigating emotional pain. Scripture is not used as a bandage to cover wounds but as a framework to understand them, and as a lifeline to anchor hope.

For those like John, daily Scripture meditation didn't remove the pain, but it created a rhythm—a steady reminder that God's presence endures through every emotional storm. When Sarah began her gratitude journal, it wasn't about pretending everything was fine. It was about slowly shifting her attention to what was still good, still beautiful, still trustworthy in her life—even when so much had been lost.

The passages shared—like Jeremiah 29:11 and Matthew 11:28—aren't quoted to preach, but to comfort. They remind you that your healing is seen by God, that your future is not over, and that rest is still available even when your world feels weary. Faith, here, is not used to minimize pain—it's offered as a safe place to bring it.

The role of surrender—especially for those like Emily and David—is also key. Their frustration with the timing of their healing mirrors what so many feel: Why isn't this happening faster? Why am I still struggling? But their stories show the quiet strength that comes when we stop striving for instant healing and start trusting in the deeper process God may be working beneath the surface.

Insight 6: Emotional Intelligence and the Power of the Pause

Another powerful insight that emerges is the role of emotional intelligence—the ability to name your emotions, reflect on them, and respond thoughtfully. Emotional intelligence isn't about suppressing feelings; it's about slowing down long enough to understand them.

This is where practices like the 90-second pause, journaling, and cognitive reframing become transformative. When Samantha and Tom committed to pausing before reacting, they noticed their conversations changed. Less reactivity. More clarity. Less blaming. More curiosity. That simple pause created space for empathy to grow and for old narratives to be challenged.

The book shows how emotional intelligence can be learned, even if it wasn't modeled growing up. Through exercises like the "Feel-Think-Do" method or daily check-ins, we retrain our brains to process emotion in real time, rather than letting it take over. Over time, this leads to healthier communication, more productive conflict resolution, and stronger relational trust.

You don't have to master it all at once. But every pause, every moment of emotional reflection, becomes a step toward a more grounded, connected life.

Insight 7: The Role of Community in Healing

Healing doesn't happen in isolation. That message rings clear throughout the entire book. We may be tempted to retreat, to figure things out on our own—but connection is what ultimately helps us feel safe enough to grow.

The stories of Lisa and Mark are especially powerful here. Both found strength and clarity not in solitude, but in the presence of others who understood. Support groups, faith-based communities, and emotionally safe friendships became places where they could share their stories without shame—and in that sharing, find healing.

There's something sacred about being seen and known in your struggle. Not fixed, not judged—just gently accompanied. The book invites you to find (or build) those communities. Whether through group counseling, faith circles, or trusted friendships, we are reminded that growth accelerates when we are not alone.

Insight 8: Parenting with Emotional Awareness

Parenting is one of the most emotionally revealing experiences we can have. Our children often trigger the very wounds we haven't yet healed. But they also give us the chance to break generational cycles and create something better.

Sarah's experience as a mother highlights this beautifully. Instead of reacting with shame or control when her child became overwhelmed, she took a breath, repaired the rupture, and modeled emotional regulation. It wasn't perfect—but it was powerful. In that moment, she didn't just help her child feel safe—she rewrote part of her own story as well.

John and Melissa's story also reflects how structure and routine—combined with emotional check-ins—can transform a chaotic home into one filled with calm and connection. The goal isn't to be flawless parents. It's to be emotionally present ones.

The message here is clear: even if you didn't grow up with emotional safety, you can create it now—for yourself, and for your children. Through intentional practices like family rituals, feeling charts, and open communication, families can develop a legacy of connection, understanding, and resilience.

Insight 9: Breaking the Shame Cycle

Underneath so many of our emotional struggles is shame—the belief that we are unworthy, unlovable, or irreparably broken. Shame doesn't just make us feel bad—it isolates us. It convinces us that our pain must be hidden, our flaws concealed, and our needs ignored.

But this book offers a different way. Through stories like Michael and Lisa's, we see how self-compassion—not perfection—is the way out of the shame spiral. Instead of beating themselves up for their emotions or reactions, they began to speak to themselves with kindness. Positive self-talk, journaling, and faith-based reflection became tools for dismantling the lies shame had built over the years.

Healing, in this view, is not about proving your worth—it's about remembering it.

Insight 10: Embracing Growth as a Daily Practice

In the end, the book's message is deeply encouraging: emotional health is not a goal you achieve once—it's a practice you commit to daily. Every small action matters. Every moment of reflection, every time you pause instead of react, every decision to forgive, to journal, to breathe—it all adds up.

Healing is made up of ordinary choices. Sharing a feeling instead of hiding it. Asking for help instead of powering through. Setting a boundary instead of people-pleasing.

These are the quiet revolutions that lead to emotional freedom.

And most importantly, the book reminds you: it's never too late. Your emotional story is still being written. The past may have shaped you, but it doesn't have to control your future.

You now have the tools. You have the strength. And now, you have the invitation—to keep going.

Part 7
Grounding and Coping Strategies

I've included this final section—a list of grounding and coping strategies—as a supportive reference for you or your loved ones as you work through emotional reasoning and dysregulation. My hope is that you'll take time to explore these tools, find the ones that resonate with you, and practice them regularly. That way, when distress arises, you'll already have what you need at hand to bring calm, clarity, and strength to the moment.

Basic Grounding Strategies

A *grounding strategy* is a practical technique used to help individuals reconnect with the present moment when they are feeling overwhelmed by distressing emotions, anxiety, or traumatic memories. These strategies work by shifting focus away from internal distress and toward the external, physical world—often through the senses, movement, or mindful awareness.

Grounding is helpful because it reduces emotional intensity, helps regulate the nervous system, and creates a sense of stability and safety. By anchoring the mind in the "here and now," grounding techniques empower individuals to manage difficult feelings without becoming consumed by them.

5-4-3-2-1 Sensory Grounding

A classic grounding technique using the five senses to bring focus to the present moment.

Steps:

1. **Name 5 things you can see** – Look around and say five things you can visually identify.

2. **Name 4 things you can feel** – Notice the texture of clothing, the floor beneath your feet, or your hands on your lap.

3. **Name 3 things you can hear** – Listen for ambient sounds like a ticking clock, traffic, or your own breathing.

4. **Name 2 things you can smell** – If nothing comes to mind, try smelling your shirt, a pen, or something nearby.

5. **Name 1 thing you can taste** – Focus on any lingering taste in your mouth or take a sip of water or bite of food.

Grounding Object (Touchstone Technique)

Using a physical object to redirect focus and create a sense of safety.

Steps:

1. Choose a small, portable item that feels comforting (e.g., smooth stone, keychain, coin).
2. Carry it with you or keep it in a familiar place.
3. When distressed, hold the object and focus your attention on:

- Its temperature
- Its texture
- Its weight
- Any associated memories or meanings

4. Breathe deeply and let the sensation anchor you to the present.

Name and Describe (Verbal Labeling)

Putting words to your surroundings or feelings to engage the logical brain.

Steps:

1. Look around your environment and describe out loud (or silently) what you see in detail.

    Example: "There is a brown desk. The surface is smooth. A blue pen is resting on the left corner."

2. Name your emotional state: "I'm feeling anxious right now."

3. Remind yourself: "I am safe. This feeling will pass. I am here, in this moment."

Body Scan

A mindfulness practice that helps reconnect with the body and reduce emotional overwhelm.

Steps:

1. Sit or lie down in a quiet space.
2. Close your eyes and take a few slow, deep breaths.
3. Start at your feet and notice any sensations (tingling, pressure, pain, warmth).
4. Move your attention slowly up your body: legs, hips, stomach, chest, arms, neck, head.
5. As you scan each area, try to release any tension you notice.
6. End with a few deep breaths, and gently bring your attention back to the room.

Mental Categories

Engaging your brain in cognitive tasks to shift attention away from distress.

Steps:

1. Pick a category such as animals, movies, sports teams, or cities.
2. Name as many items as you can in that category.
    - Example: "Dog, cat, rabbit, elephant, giraffe…"

3. For added distraction, use the alphabet (e.g., "Animals A–Z").

4. Keep going until your emotional intensity lowers.

Movement-Based Grounding

Using physical movement to reconnect to the present and release stored tension.

Steps:

1. Stand up and stretch your arms overhead, then down to your toes.

2. March in place or walk slowly around the room, noticing each step.

3. Press your feet into the ground and feel the floor beneath you.

4. Gently tap your arms or legs or do light jumping jacks.

5. Focus on the physical sensations: heart rate, muscle movement, body temperature.

Breathwork Techniques

Breathwork in counseling refers to intentional breathing techniques used to calm the body and mind during emotional distress or trauma recovery. When a person experiences anxiety, panic, or trauma triggers, their breathing often becomes shallow and rapid, signaling the body's stress response.

Breathwork helps by slowing and deepening the breath, which activates the parasympathetic nervous system—the body's natural calming mechanism. This reduces heart rate, lowers cortisol levels, and promotes a sense of safety. In trauma counseling, breathwork is especially valuable because it gives clients a simple, accessible tool to regulate emotions, stay grounded, and regain control during overwhelming moments.

Diaphragmatic Breathing (Deep Belly Breathing)

A foundational technique that promotes full oxygen exchange and activates the relaxation response.

How to do it:

1. Sit or lie down comfortably.
2. Place one hand on your chest and one on your belly.
3. Inhale slowly through your nose for 4–5 seconds, allowing your belly to rise while your chest stays relatively still.
4. Exhale slowly through your mouth for 6–7 seconds, feeling your belly fall.
5. Repeat for 5–10 cycles.

Why it helps:

It lowers heart rate, relaxes the nervous system, and reduces anxiety symptoms.

Box Breathing (Square Breathing)

A structured method used to restore calm and focus, often used in high-stress environments.

How to do it:

1. Inhale through your nose for 4 seconds.
2. Hold your breath for 4 seconds.
3. Exhale through your mouth for 4 seconds.
4. Hold again for 4 seconds.
5. Repeat the full cycle for 4–5 minutes.

Why it helps:

The even rhythm helps reset the breath, calm the mind, and reduce panic or overwhelm.

4-7-8 Breathing

A relaxing breath technique that helps quiet the mind and body, especially before sleep or during emotional dysregulation.

How to do it:

1. Inhale through your nose for 4 seconds.
2. Hold the breath for 7 seconds.
3. Exhale slowly through your mouth for 8 seconds.
4. Repeat up to 4 cycles.

Why it helps:

It slows the heart rate and increases oxygen intake, creating a deep calming effect.

Pursed-Lip Breathing

Often used to reduce shortness of breath and calm anxiety by regulating exhalation. I learned this from my own respiratory therapist years ago and find that it is one of the best methods for breathing toward calmness.

How to do it:

1. Inhale through your nose for 2–3 seconds.
2. Purse your lips as if blowing out a candle.
3. Exhale slowly and gently through pursed lips for 4–6 seconds.
4. Repeat until breathing slows and steadies.

Why it helps:

It extends exhalation, which helps expel carbon dioxide and reduce tension in the body.

Alternate Nostril Breathing

A yogic technique used to balance the nervous system and enhance focus and calm.

How to do it:

1. Sit comfortably and use your right thumb to close your right nostril.
2. Inhale slowly through your left nostril.

3. Close your left nostril with your ring finger and release your thumb from the right nostril.

4. Exhale through the right nostril.

5. Inhale through the right nostril, then close it and exhale through the left.

6. Continue alternating for several minutes.

Why it helps:

Calms by diverting focus on to a task that is rhythmic and measured.

Body Movement Techniques

Progressive Muscle Relaxation (PMR)

A tension-release technique that helps bring awareness to the body and promotes deep relaxation.

How to do it:

1. Find a quiet, comfortable space to sit or lie down.

2. Starting with your feet, tense the muscles tightly for 5–10 seconds.

3. Release the tension slowly while noticing the difference between tension and relaxation.

4. Move upward through your body (legs, abdomen, chest, arms, shoulders, face), repeating the tension-release cycle.

5. Finish with a few deep breaths.

Why it helps:

Releases stored physical tension and brings attention back to the body, calming the nervous system.

Grounding Walk (Mindful Walking)

A slow, intentional walk that combines physical movement with present-moment awareness.

How to do it:

1. Walk slowly and deliberately, ideally in a quiet or natural setting.
2. Pay attention to the sensation of your feet connecting with the ground.
3. Notice what you see, hear, feel, and smell as you walk.
4. Focus on the rhythm of your steps and breathing.
5. If your mind wanders, gently return focus to your steps.

Why it helps:

Integrates body and mind, reduces anxiety, and supports mindfulness and grounding.

Self-Tapping (Butterfly Hug)

A bilateral stimulation technique often used in trauma recovery to promote calm and self-regulation.

How to do it:

1. Cross your arms over your chest with fingertips resting just below your collarbones.
2. Gently tap your hands alternately on your upper arms or shoulders, left then right.
3. Breathe deeply and slowly as you tap, continuing for 1–2 minutes.
4. Focus on the rhythm or repeat calming phrases silently as you tap.

Why it helps:

Stimulates both brain hemispheres, reduces stress, and provides a comforting self-soothing gesture.

Stretching and Movement Flow

Gentle, guided stretches that help release tension and re-center the body and mind.

How to do it:

1. Begin in a standing or seated position.
2. Slowly stretch your arms overhead and reach side to side.
3. Roll your shoulders, twist gently at the waist, or bend forward to touch your toes.
4. Move through each stretch slowly and with intention, connecting to your breath.
5. End with a long full-body stretch and a few deep breaths.

Why it helps:

Releases physical stress and encourages present-moment awareness through mindful movement.

Rhythmic Movement or Rocking

Repetitive, soothing motion that mimics early attachment soothing and helps regulate the nervous system.

How to do it:

1. Sit in a rocking chair or on the floor, or stand and gently sway side to side.
2. Focus on creating a steady, calming rhythm.
3. Breathe deeply as you move, allowing the rhythm to guide your breath.
4. Optionally pair the movement with a calming word, prayer, or mantra.
5. Continue for several minutes until you feel calmer.

Why it helps:

Activates the body's innate calming response and can be particularly soothing for those with trauma or sensory sensitivity.

Empty Chair Technique for Self-Soothing and Emotional Processing at Home

The *empty chair technique* is a form of **gestalt therapy** that helps individuals express and process difficult emotions by imagining a person, part of themselves, or an emotion sitting in an empty chair. This technique can be used **at**

home alone to promote self-soothing, emotional release, and inner clarity.

Why It Helps:

- Offers a safe outlet to express unresolved feelings
- Helps process grief, anger, anxiety, or inner conflict
- Encourages self-compassion and emotional regulation
- Builds insight and closure by externalizing thoughts and emotions

How to Set It Up:

1. Choose a private, quiet space.
2. Place **two chairs** facing each other—one for you, and one left empty.
3. Decide who or what the empty chair represents (e.g., another person, a part of yourself, or an emotion).
4. Sit in your chair and begin speaking aloud or silently, as if that person or part were sitting in front of you.
5. You may switch chairs to speak from the other perspective if helpful.

Examples of How to Use the Empty Chair at Home:

To Process Unresolved Conflict or Hurt

Use: Speak to someone who hurt you or whom you miss (e.g., a parent, ex-partner, or deceased loved one).

Steps:

- Sit in your chair and say what you wish you could say to them: "You really hurt me when you…"
- Express emotions without holding back.
- If needed, switch chairs and respond as that person, imagining their possible reply.
- Return to your chair and continue until emotions feel more settled.

To Confront a Part of Yourself (Inner Critic or Wounded Child)

Use: Talk to a part of yourself you are struggling with—like your inner critic, a fearful version of you, or your younger self.

Steps:

- Assign the empty chair to that part of you (e.g., "This is the part of me that feels like a failure").
- Speak directly: "I know you're trying to protect me, but you're also hurting me."
- Offer understanding or reassurance.

- Switch chairs if you want to speak *as* that part and express its perspective.
- End with compassionate self-talk: "I'm listening to you, and I'm going to take care of us."

To Externalize an Emotion (e.g., Anxiety, Anger, Depression)

Use: Separate from overwhelming emotions by giving them a "voice" and a place to sit.

Steps:

- Say, "Anxiety, you can sit over there. I see you."
- Speak to it: "Why are you here today? What are you trying to tell me?"
- Listen to your intuition and respond with grounding thoughts: "You don't need to control me. I'm safe."
- You can even visualize asking the emotion to leave or shrink in size.

To Practice Forgiveness or Letting Go

Use: Talk to someone from the past to express forgiveness or release lingering pain.

Steps:

- Sit facing the empty chair and say, "I've carried this long enough…"
- Express the pain fully, then say: "I choose to release this. Not for you, but for me."

- End with a symbolic gesture—stand up and walk away, light a candle, or take a deep breath to mark closure.

To Rehearse a Hard Conversation

Use: Practice setting boundaries, asking for help, or having a difficult discussion with someone in your life.

Steps:

- Visualize the person in the chair.
- Speak your truth: "I need to talk about something that's been on my heart…"
- Rehearse staying calm and clear.
- Imagine their possible responses and practice staying grounded in your message.

Tips for Doing Empty Chair Effectively:

- Speak aloud if possible—it helps externalize emotions.
- Don't worry about "doing it right"—the goal is expression, not perfection.
- Use deep breathing before and after to regulate your nervous system.
- Journal your experience afterward to reflect and reinforce insights.

What Is "Acting As If"?

The *"Acting As If"* technique encourages individuals to intentionally behave as if they are already feeling, thinking, or living in a more positive or calm state—even if they don't yet fully believe it. It's based on the idea that behavior can influence emotion and thought, not just the other way around.

By temporarily adopting a posture, mindset, or behavior that reflects a healthier or more regulated version of yourself, you can begin to *shift your internal state* toward greater calm, confidence, and emotional control.

Why It's Helpful:

- Creates new mental and emotional patterns through behavior
- Helps break the cycle of emotional paralysis or distress
- Empowers clients to act in alignment with their values rather than their emotions
- Can be especially effective when feeling anxious, overwhelmed, insecure, or emotionally stuck

Examples of How to Use "Acting As If" for Self-Soothing or Calming:

Acting as if You Feel Calm

Use: When you're feeling overwhelmed or panicky.

- How to do it:

- Sit or stand tall, drop your shoulders, and slow your breathing intentionally.
- Speak slowly and gently to yourself: "I am calm and in control."
- Move deliberately and unhurriedly, as someone who feels grounded would.
- Smile gently, even if you don't feel like it.
- Practice for 5–10 minutes, letting your body lead your brain toward calm.

Acting as if You Are Confident

Use: When you're anxious, insecure, or facing a challenge.

How to do it:

- Straighten your posture and make eye contact with yourself in a mirror.
- Say: "I've done hard things before—I can do this too."
- Walk into a room as if you belong there, even if you feel nervous.
- Choose an action that a confident version of you would take—speak up, set a boundary, or try something new.

Acting as if You Are Emotionally Safe

Use: When triggered by past trauma or feeling emotionally unsafe.

How to do it:

- Place your hand over your heart or hug yourself.
- Look around and name three things that show you are safe right now.
- Move with the rhythm of safety—soft, slow, grounded.
- Say aloud: "I am here now. I am safe. I am cared for."
- Act with trust in the moment, even if your body feels on edge.

Acting as if You Are Already Coping Well

Use: When overwhelmed by fear or stuck in hopelessness.

How to do it:

- Ask: "What would I be doing right now if I were handling this well?"
- Do one small task that aligns with coping—make tea, take a shower, write a plan.
- Imagine being your future self who already made it through this.
- Begin to act in small ways as if that version of you is already present.

Acting as if You Are Self-Compassionate

Use: When experiencing self-criticism, shame, or regret.

How to do it:

- Sit quietly and speak to yourself as you would to a hurting friend: "It's okay to struggle. I'm learning."

- Wrap yourself in a blanket, light a candle, or engage in a kind gesture toward yourself.

- Choose one action that reflects kindness, even if your inner critic resists it—rest, journal, forgive.

Tips for Practicing "Acting As If":

- You don't have to *feel* it yet—just *practice* it.

- Keep it small and believable to start—one behavior, one phrase, one posture.

- Use a mirror or visualization to embody the version of yourself you're acting from.

- Reflect afterward: "How did that feel? What shifted in me?"

What Is Thought Reframing and Disputing?

Thought reframing and disputing is a CBT-based technique that helps clients manage distressing emotions by identifying negative or irrational thoughts, challenging their accuracy, and replacing them with more balanced, helpful alternatives.

When emotions spiral, they are often fueled by distorted or exaggerated beliefs (e.g., "I can't handle this," or "I'm a failure"). Reframing helps calm the emotional response by reshaping the inner dialogue with truth, logic, and self-compassion.

Why It's Helpful:

- Reduces anxiety, shame, anger, and overwhelm
- Builds self-awareness and emotional regulation
- Interrupts automatic negative thought patterns
- Empowers the client to speak truth to inner lies or distortions
- Supports a growth mindset and self-compassion

How to Use Thought Reframing & Disputing:

1. Notice the Distressing Thought

Ask: "What am I thinking right now that's making me feel worse?"

Example: "I'm never going to get this right."

2. Name the Emotion That Follows

Identify the feeling triggered by the thought.

Example: "This thought makes me feel hopeless and anxious."

3. Challenge the Thought (Dispute It)

Ask questions like:

- Is this 100% true?
- What evidence do I have for and against it?
- Is there another way to look at this?
- Would I say this to a friend going through the same thing?

4. Reframe the Thought

    Replace it with a more accurate, compassionate, or balanced perspective.

    Example: "I've made mistakes before, but I've also figured things out. I can take one step at a time."

5. Check in with Your Emotions

    Notice how your emotional state shifts after the reframe.

    Ask: *"How do I feel now after thinking this new thought?"*

Examples of Reframing & Disputing in Action:

Negative Thought:

"I can't do anything right."

Dispute & Reframe:

- Is that really true all the time?
- What have I done well in the past week?
- New Thought: "I'm having a tough moment, but that doesn't define me. I've succeeded before, and I will again."

Negative Thought:

"If I feel anxious, it means I'm weak."

Dispute & Reframe:

- Is anxiety a sign of weakness—or of being human?
- Would I judge a friend for feeling this way?

- New Thought: "Anxiety is a normal response. Facing it takes courage, not weakness."

Negative Thought:

"No one really cares about me."

Dispute & Reframe:

- Am I overlooking the people who have shown they care?
- Could this be the depression talking, not the truth?
- New Thought: "I feel lonely right now, but I do have people who care—even if it's hard to see in this moment."

Negative Thought:

"I'll never get through this."

Dispute & Reframe:

- What evidence do I have that I won't survive this?
- Have I ever overcome something hard before?
- New Thought: "This is difficult, but I've made it through tough things before. I don't have to have all the answers right now."

Negative Thought:

"I shouldn't feel this way."

Dispute & Reframe:

- Who says I shouldn't? What rule is that based on?

- Is it okay to feel? What would compassion look like here?
- New Thought: "It's okay to feel what I feel. My emotions are signals, not flaws."

Tips for Practicing Thought Reframing:

- Write your thoughts and disputes in a journal for clarity.
- Use a "Thought Record Sheet" (trigger → thought → feeling → challenge → reframe).
- Practice often—even if it feels unnatural at first. Reframing gets easier with repetition.
- Be gentle with yourself—don't force positivity, aim for balance and truth.

Fair Fighting Rules for Conflicted Couples.

Sometimes, it is vital to have some rules in place before a conflict arises, so that you and your spouse know what to do when emotional reasoning overtakes the conflict. John Gottman[11] has written extensively on the nature of language used in conflict and how choices of words and their use affects the outcome. Below are some fair fighting rules you and your spouse might agree on before you need them, just in case.

1. Take Time to Calm Down First

- Don't try to resolve conflict in the heat of emotional overwhelm.
- Use a 20- to 30-minute break to self-soothe and return when both partners feel more regulated.

- Agree in advance on a signal or phrase like "I need a pause" to request time-out without blame.

Fight the Problem, Not the Person

- Keep the focus on the issue—not character attacks, past mistakes, or personality flaws.
- Use language that describes your experience instead of assigning blame.
- Instead of "You're so selfish," say, "I felt hurt when I didn't feel considered."

Use "I" Statements, Not "You" Accusations

- Speak from your own feelings and needs.
- Example: "I feel lonely when we don't spend time together," vs. "You never make time for me."

Stick to One Issue at a Time

- Avoid "kitchen sinking" (bringing up multiple past issues).
- Focus on resolving one disagreement rather than opening emotional floodgates.

No Name-Calling, Mocking, or Sarcasm

- These are forms of contempt and will quickly escalate conflict.
- Agree to no belittling, eye-rolling, or tone of voice that signals superiority.

Stay in the Present—Don't Dig Up the Past

- Avoid rehashing unrelated past mistakes to win an argument.
- If the past needs to be addressed, save it for a separate, intentional discussion.

Practice Listening Without Interrupting

- Take turns. One speaks, the other listens without defending.
- Use reflective listening: "What I hear you saying is…" before responding.

Check the Story You're Telling Yourself

- Emotional reasoning can distort perceptions (e.g., "If I feel unloved, it must mean I am unloved").
- Pause and ask: "Is there another way to interpret this?"

Assume Good Intentions

- Begin with the belief that your partner is not your enemy.
- Remind yourself: "They're struggling too" or "They're not trying to hurt me."

Agree to Repair and Reconnect

- When things go wrong, own your part and offer repair attempts:
- "That came out wrong—can I try again?"
- "I didn't mean to shut you down. I want to understand."

- Accept and respond to repair attempts graciously when offered.

Use Gentle Starts, Not Harsh Criticism

- The way a conflict starts often determines how it ends.
- Start softly: "Can we talk about something that's been on my mind?" instead of launching into blame.

Know When to Pause and Revisit Later

- If either partner becomes flooded, it's okay to reschedule the conversation.
- Say: "I care about this, and I want to give it my best attention—can we try again after we calm down?"

Use Physical Grounding or Soothing Techniques If Triggered

- Agree that either person may use grounding tools (deep breathing, stepping away, using a fidget, etc.) during difficult conversations.

Validate Before You Problem-Solve

- Emotional immaturity often results in defensiveness. Validation helps disarm that.
- Example: "I get why you'd feel that way. That makes sense."

Seek Understanding, Not Just Agreement

- You may not always agree, but you can seek to understand your partner's point of view.

- "Help me understand what's really important to you about this."

SELECTED REFERENCES

Bradshaw, J. (1988). *Bradshaw on: The family—A new way of creating solid self-esteem.* Health Communications.
This foundational book explores how dysfunctional family systems impact identity, boundaries, and emotional development. Bradshaw offers insights into breaking generational patterns and cultivating a healthier sense of self.

Bradshaw, J. (1990). *Homecoming: Reclaiming and championing your inner child.* Bantam Books.
Bradshaw's landmark work on inner child healing provides practical steps to confront and heal from childhood emotional wounds, restoring authenticity and emotional balance in adulthood.

Bradshaw, J. (2005). *Healing the shame that binds you.* Health Communications.
Originally published in 1988, this influential book reveals how toxic shame develops and perpetuates dysfunction. Bradshaw explains how healing shame is key to personal growth and relational health.

Goleman, D. (1995). *Emotional intelligence: Why it can matter more than IQ.* Bantam Books.
Introduces the concept of the "amygdala hijack" and explores the role of emotional intelligence in personal and professional success.

Porges, S. W. (2011). *The polyvagal theory: Neurophysiological foundations of emotions,*

attachment, communication, and self-regulation. **W. W. Norton & Company.**
An in-depth scientific exploration of how the autonomic nervous system influences emotional regulation, trauma responses, and social engagement.

Shapiro, B. (n.d.). *Facts don't care about your feelings* **[Phrase]. Frequently used in public commentary and media. Retrieved from** https://www.dailywire.com
A cultural phrase popularized by commentator Ben Shapiro. This book's title and framework are offered as a complementary perspective focused on emotional healing and relational growth.

Siegel, D. J. (1999). *The developing mind: How relationships and the brain interact to shape who we are.* **Guilford Press.**
Introduces the "Window of Tolerance" concept and explains how early experiences shape brain development and emotional regulation.

Walker, P. (2013). *Complex PTSD: From surviving to thriving.* **Azure Coyote Publishing.**
Presents the "fawn" response in trauma theory and provides insight into emotional healing for survivors of complex trauma.

About the Author

Dr. Chuck Carrington, PhD, EdS, MA, is a Christian therapist, educator, author, and speaker with over 30 years of experience working with couples, families, and individuals—including trauma survivors, foster families and children, men recovering from pornography addiction, and the wives healing from betrayal trauma. He specializes in trauma, grief, and loss, with a focused practice in Christian counseling that emphasizes relational restoration in the wake of betrayal, infidelity, and emotional dysfunction.

Dr. Chuck's research explores innovative approaches to loss recovery, process addictions, betrayal trauma, post-traumatic embitterment, and the long-term impact of childhood family dysfunction. Blending biblical wisdom with evidence-based therapeutic models and a down-to-earth relational style, he brings compassion, clarity, and deep insight into how past wounds shape present relationships.

He is the founder of *Connect Christian Family Counseling*, where he walks alongside clients on their journey toward emotional and relational wholeness.

When he's not writing or counseling, Dr. Chuck enjoys reading, researching, leading workshops, and serving in local ministry projects. He also hosts free online support and discipleship groups. This book reflects his passion for bringing a practical, gospel-centered message to those navigating the complex challenges of modern life—helping them rediscover their identity and purpose in God's redemptive plan, and equipping them to grow in truth, strength, and grace.

If You Need Counseling or Help,

Dr Chuck offers Christian Faith-Based Counseling and Coaching in men's recovery from porn and cyber-addiction, Betrayal Trauma recovery for women, and restorative counseling to help heal and recover marriages after betrayal.

For a consultation via telehealth video, contact Dr Chuck to get more information on how to overcome the damage of betrayal and addiction. Use the website below to sign up for recovery and support groups, or to join Dr Chuck's online psychoeducational programs.

If you are looking for marriage enhancement counseling or coaching, Dr Chuck offers online webinars and forums to help Christian couples explore their marriage, and how it conforms to God's plan for marriage, to find forgiveness and healing, or to plan for an extraordinary marriage from the outset for engaged couples.

Believers should ask for the Faith-based community discount for the best possible pricing. Free groups include Healing Hearts for women damaged by betrayal, Overcomer's Group for men struggling with porn addiction and cyber addiction.

www.connectcounselor.com
Connect Christian Family Counseling
757 965-5450

Other Titles by Dr Chuck

The Renewed Mind: Rebuilding Trust in Marriage by Overcoming Porn Addiction for Life
ISBN# 979-89892386-3-7
Is available on Amazon at
https://a.co/d/7qwOY7h

The Renewed Mind companion workbook
ISBN# 979-8-9892386-2-0 is available on Amazon at
https://a.co/d/fTPdxoO

The Loving Marriage: Jesus Reduce Me To Love. Lessons on living out 1 Corinthians in Marriage is available on Amazon https://a.co/d/eZttPf8
ISBN# 979-8989238651

Check out Dr Chuck's *Seven Greatest Hits in Marriage Counseling*, a series of video supported coaching modules presenting his most effective tools to help couples exceed a typical marriage.

www.connectcounselor.com
Connect Christian Family Counseling
757 965-5450
DrChuck@connectcounselor.com
https://connectcounselor.com/group-counseling/

REFERENCES

[1] Shapiro, B. (n.d.). *Facts don't care about your feelings* [Phrase]. Frequently used in public commentary and media. Retrieved from https://www.dailywire.com

[2] Bradshaw, J. (1990). *Homecoming: reclaiming and championing your inner child.* Bantam Books.

[3] Goleman, D. (1995). *Emotional intelligence: Why it can matter more than IQ.* Bantam Books.

[4] Bradshaw, J. (1988). *Bradshaw on: The family—A new way of creating solid self-esteem.* Health Communications.

Bradshaw, J. (1990). *Homecoming: Reclaiming and championing your inner child.* Bantam Books.

Bradshaw, J. (2005). *Healing the shame that binds you.* Health Communications.

[5] Walker, Pete. *Complex PTSD: From Surviving to Thriving.* Azure Coyote Publishing, 2013.

[6] Porges, S. W. (2011). *The polyvagal theory: Neurophysiological foundations of emotions, attachment, communication, and self-regulation.* W. W. Norton & Company.

[7] Siegel, D. J. (1999). *The developing mind: How relationships and the brain interact to shape who we are.* Guilford Press.

[8] Taylor, J. B. (2008). My stroke of insight: A brain scientist's personal journey. Viking.

[9] Neff, K. D. (2003). Self-compassion: An alternative conceptualization of a healthy attitude toward oneself. Self and Identity, 2(2), 175-192

[10] Perry, B. D., & Winfrey, O. (2021). What happened to you?: Conversations on trauma, resilience, and healing. Flatiron Books.

[11] Gottman, John M. (1994). *Why marriages succeed or fail and how you can make yours last.* New York: Simon and Schuster.

www.ingramcontent.com/pod-product-compliance
Lightning Source LLC
Chambersburg PA
CBHW072013150426
43194CB00008B/1089